MW01061768

Raising Thinking Children and Teens

Raising Thinking Children (Courtesy of Angela Browne-Miller)

Raising Thinking Children and Teens

Guiding Mental and Moral Development

ANGELA BROWNE-MILLER

PRAEGER
An Imprint of ABC-CLIO, LLC

A B C   C L I O

Santa Barbara, California • Denver, Colorado • Oxford, England

Library of Congress Cataloging-in-Publication Data
Browne-Miller, Angela, 1952–
  Raising thinking children and teens: guiding mental and moral development / Angela Browne-Miller.
    p. cm.
  Includes bibliographical references and index.
  ISBN 978-0-313-35876-0 (hard copy : alk. paper) —
ISBN 978-0-313-35877-7 (ebook)
  1. Child rearing. 2. Child development 3. Metacognition in children.
I. Title.
  HQ769.B686   2009
  649′.12—dc22   2009005378

13 12 11 10 9   1 2 3 4 5

This book is also available on the World Wide Web as an eBook.
Visit www.abc-clio.com for details.

ABC-CLIO, LLC
130 Cremona Drive, P.O. Box 1911
Santa Barbara, California 93116–1911

This book is printed on acid-free paper ∞

Manufactured in the United States of America

To the children in our family line, and in the human family line.

Contents

Foreword

It is common for an expert in a field related to a book to write its foreword. I choose to break with tradition here, as I am not an expert, per say. I do not have children of my own yet, nor do I have extensive education in children's studies. However, being someone's daughter, maybe I *am* an expert on the material in this book based on my own experiences growing up. And furthermore, being the author's daughter, I have lived the development and testing of the material in this book over the years, beginning when I was a baby, and I may thus have earned an additional level of expertise.

In fact, I learned the word, metacognition, a concept that you will read about in this book, at the age of four when my mother was conducting research on intelligence and learning processes. Metacognition intrigued me already at that young age. The idea that we could think about thinking while we were thinking something, or solving a problem, fascinated me. I continued to think about thinking processes as I grew up and continue to see the importance in this sort of awareness. When my mother asked me to write the foreword for this book, I couldn't refuse, especially having experienced first hand many of the learning experiences she writes about.

This book offers both simple and profound insights into almost every aspect of raising a child, from infancy into young adulthood. It touches base with parenting tools I was aware of when my mother applied them, such as encouraging a child to think about the thinking process itself or understanding problem solving. This book also encompasses ideas I wouldn't have considered before, but will definitely apply when I have my own children, such as what to look for when deciding on a preschool or day care facility.

The way this book frames the insights it provides moves the reader into a new perspective on what it means to raise a child, and what it means to be part of raising the next generation. Clearly, every second in a young person's life is one that matters. Parents, teachers, and policy makers everywhere will benefit from this discussion of what it means to raise thinking children and teens.

Certainly parents can benefit from this friendly, easy to read, rich book, full of the sort of advice you would get from parents and grandparents as well from child and teen development specialists. The rich level of detail applied to the various subjects in this book is presented in simple-to-understand discussions that will allow parents or anyone involved in raising a child to apply these ideas and methods in their own lives. In the beginning of this book, you will read about the "basic rules" of parenting. Although at first glance these rules may seem obvious, I am sure that they often get lost in the hustle and bustle of parenthood. Therefore the first portion of this book serves as a gentle reminder to help parents stay on track, not only for their children but also for themselves.

One of the things that I have found most beneficial in reading this book is that it caused me to think through my own childhood. I was able to relive instances from the years when I was growing up, and to see an adult's perspective on why my parents did what they did. For example, my mother repeated some things quite obviously, all the while telling me she was purposely repeating herself. As we are all aware, children learn from repetition, but looking back, did I know this was how I was learning? Only when my mother explained it to me (which she did, over and over), and showed me that if she taught me something once, then the same thing again, and then again, that the third time, I would understand it best. My understanding would increase as the succession continued. As I got older, and my mother efficiently scoped out each afterschool program, was I confused at the thorough level of her interest? Yes. Why couldn't I just go to a class without it being checked out first? In retrospect, and through reading this book, I see that this was a regular precaution that all parents must take when involving their children in a new facility and program.

As I move into the time in my life when more and more of my friends are becoming parents, having children of my own is approaching the forefront of my consciousness. I think about where I will want to live in the future, not only based on my own needs but also based on what I know of the schools in that area. What is the surrounding environment like? How safe are the neighborhoods and the parks, and how influential will they be on my child's development? As I feel myself and see my friends becoming more aware of these issues, the relevance of this book becomes more and more clear. I would be proud to hand this book to any parent, and to any friend of mine who already has children or is hopeful of having them in the future.

Evacheska deAngelis

Acknowledgments

I wish to thank many people for the inspiration to write this handbook on raising thinking children and teens. Most of all, I would like to thank my daughter, Evacheska deAngelis, for the inspiration and life lessons that she has provided me from the moment she was born (if not before) right up to this day, and on into the future as well. What a privilege it always is, and has been all along, to share my thoughts on learning and on life with Evacheska. And how exciting it was to see that I could teach my child what metacognition might be, that children could understand this concept I love so much— *thinking about thinking*—which I write about especially in the later chapters of this book. Every step of the way, my daughter has been my teacher. And now, I have been additionally gifted with my daughter's editing of this book, which is quite fitting as she has shown me what it means to raise a thinking child. Evacheska, thank you, you see so much, you are such a gift.

And there are so many others who have been there at steps along the way. Certainly one of them is Martha Kendrick Ketmer, Esq. in Washington, D.C., who mentored me long ago when I was an intern in Washington, D.C. Martha's wise and caring role modeling has stayed with me throughout my adulthood, and I have been able to share what she offered me with many others. Martha, thank you for sharing yourself at the right moment in my life.

My multilingual parents, who always said, "Go to school, and then when you come home, we will teach you something," showed me how to draw, how to solve problems, how to love music, how to understand thinking in many languages. My mother taught me to paint, and what it meant to appreciate color. My father showed me how precious ideas are, how deeply we can delve into our minds to pull out new understandings, Thank you so much, Louisa Francesca Mirella deAngelis and Lee Winston Browne, you left the planet far too early. I was far too young to see how important your mental workings were. I am understanding your minds better and better every day.

Systems thinker, professor, and past University of California Regent, Gregory Bateson, who years ago (when I was at UC Santa Cruz) introduced me to his theories of the "double bind" and of the "levels of learning," made a profound contribution to my thinking. He left the planet far too soon for me to thank him enough, and I thank him right now.

Systems thinker, professor, and philosopher, C. West Churchman, who sat on both of my doctoral committees at UC Berkeley and guided me into several inquires into the human mind, was such an inspiration to me. Memory of his lectures on ethics will never leave me. Memories of his decision-making processes and models have guided me in my thinking for many years now.

And I must not forget those who stood and still stand by me, as I trek this life path. Rikki Baum, Lee Brazil, Neil Gilbert, Martha Hyde, Barbara Kaufman, Maureen Manley, Ken Norris, David Parker, truly remarkable minds, friends and colleagues all. There are so many others I wish to thank, and were it not for space I would. Perhaps the best way to say thank you all for these years of fabulous friendship is to share this little handbook full of advice with everyone else.

Introduction

Astounding universes of thought, judgment and learning, vast and intricate, chaotic and orderly, foreign and familiar, are available to each and every one of us. All we have to know is how to use our minds. All we have to do is think—think well. And make good decisions.

But who will parent our mental and moral potentials into full realization? Who will guide us on the journeys of thought and judgment required to travel to such new places? In the end, we are our own captains, our own teachers. No one else can push us to those towering pinnacles of expression and achievement—to the heights of actual thought and of sound judgment of which we are each capable.

We are so alone in a world hungry for real mentors, intellectual guidance, personal tutoring in decision making, reasoning, and the science of the mind. But our children are not. They have us—their parents and teachers—their elders. They have us but for a few years before they become us.

The mind of a young person is so very precious and special. In that mind is forming the paths that future generations will travel. In that mind are indeed awesome streams of thought—mental workings so exotic that only the future will find a place for them. The wealth of mental ability locked away in a young person's mind is immeasurable. All we can do to touch it is to help that person find the key that will unlock her or his own mental vault.

Despite our great interests in education, we tend to overlook the more subtle aspects of young people's development. And we tend to overlook the links between cognitive, intellectual, creative, and moral development. Yet, it is our attitudes regarding the realization of our children's and teen's abilities that can make or break their mental and moral intelligences. The care and feeding of young people's abilities is some of the most important work we will ever do. It is some of the greatest love we will ever give. It is, perhaps, the greatest guarantee of our immortality. We live on through the next generation, which then lives on through its children.

Parenting? Yes, Then and Now (Illustration by Angela Browne-Miller)

CHAPTER **1**

Notes from the Front: Parenting Now

I cannot begin this book without first focusing on those pillars of strength and perseverance—the all important but oft forgotten parents of the children and teens we care so much about. Parents play a major role in the outcome of the birth through 18 years. Surely, parents can be overlooked by society and by each other, but what is even more concerning is that parents can overlook themselves.

I am reminded of a little incident that took place some years back. It was late in the afternoon on a gray and rainy weekday. The traffic outside was heavy, and the crowd inside the store was agitated. I stood in a line of fifteen shopping carts pushed by fifteen assorted families, mostly mothers with children under ten, formed in front of the only open check-out stand. Every one of us was eyeing with longing the other nine stands, all closed for some reason, as if the act of wishing very hard could open them. Our own checker was slow and glaring at us all, overwhelmed by the demand and angry at the burden. She looked to be about eighteen and dressed for a midnight party. Children were climbing in and out of the carts, demanding gum and candy and freedom to roam the store and run outside in the jammed up parking lot. One little boy decided to try diving out of his cart head first. He wasn't mine, but I just had to stop him.

His surprised mother thanked me profusely as she released the other two she had been restraining from beating each other up and overturning the candy stand as they did exactly that. I smiled and said something about how hard it is to manage it all these days. She laughed and said, "Well then, I guess you've met my three kids: Give Me, Buy Me, and Drive Me." I couldn't help but ask if they had a last name. She nodded a certain yes, and said,

"MORE! And more and more and more and more and more!" I have since learned that this was a joke that was making its way around the country and then on to joke heaven. But its meaning stays on for very loving but nevertheless overworked, stretched too thin, run too ragged, very working-dazed parents everywhere.

Every time we fly a major airline, we hear instructions for using the oxygen masks located above our seats. Again and again, we are told that, should there be a need for oxygen during the flight, parents must first put their masks on themselves. Only after they have done so should they address the breathing needs of their children. A few passengers—more often than not new parents and or new passengers—gulp. Most of the others barely listen anymore, these directions being so commonplace. We fly. And then we land, live on the ground, and rarely think about this rule. But, should we take this same dictum back down to the ground?

BASIC RULE NUMBER ONE: KNOW WHEN TO PUT YOURSELF FIRST AND WHEN NOT TO

A basic rule is embedded in the oxygen mask message, but what it is? When does it apply and when is it absolutely wrong? How does a parent make such choices in daily life? How do you know when to put yourself first? How do you know when to put your family first? These are basic questions many parents are actually ashamed to ask. So here we have basic rule number one: Know when to put yourself first, for everyone's sake, and when not to. After all, you have to be able to survive to save your children, and sometimes more than your children alone—your family.

And today's family is in need of your attention. Families are living things, living systems, that are under increasing social, economic, even evolutionary pressure. The pressures are so strong that the family itself may be an endangered species. In times not so long past, the family was viewed as a haven in a heartless world, an enclave of safety and protection, a primary safety net. The word "family" was evocative of such cozy images as a holiday feast, cookies baking in the oven, parents and children around a fire, the family vacation, and the veritable family picnic. Magazines, billboards, and television helped to generate the paste-up image of the so-called all-American family. We were taught what families looked like and what families did, or at least we told ourselves we knew this. Now we wonder. What are families for? And for those of us who spent years single parenting, we also asked questions such as: Aren't we families too?

But how on Earth should parents know what a family should look like? Today's family is on the front lines of massive social change and profound redefinition. The prevalence of conditions such as economic stress, job-family role strain, addiction, domestic violence, and more plague families. Parents struggle to hold their families together against career, economic, social, health, aging, gender, sexual, and other fierce pressures. Some of them make it, but there are often costs to the survival of the family. And, there are often costs to the demise of the family. But let's not call this a lose-lose situation. If you have a family, any form of family, you are spearheading a major, big-time revolution. That's all. No big deal. You captain a ship in tossing seas where the weather is always changing. Parents, welcome to the front lines of massive social change. You know this place well, even if you don't have time to stand back and see it, because you live here every day.

BASIC RULE NUMBER TWO: GET WITH THE PROGRAM—DEAL WITH REALITY

So we have no choice but to get with the program, fellow parents. This is basic rule number two: You have to deal with reality. At a certain point, we have to accept the trends, handle them face on. Don't sink. Stand up. Survive. Economic and life management pressures come at you from all directions.

In two-parent families, couples work to divide domestic and economic responsibilities, sometimes fairly, sometimes unfairly, usually in the only way they can agree or fight through on. Divorce is practically a way of life. Single parenting is fast becoming the norm. Many are parenting all alone, sole parents. Others share the job, as do their children. Children of divorce, being divided in various ways, pack bags and move from home to home, pilgrims of change on an ongoing trek back and forth between increasingly disparate realities. Is this right? Do their parents have a right to create such a reality for them? Can their parents be held responsible or is the tide of change greater than the bond between people who at one time came close enough to conceive a child?

Every parent arrives at her or his own answers to these tough questions. Regardless of a parent's answers, the realities generated amidst these dilemmas demand immediate attention, action. Drive here. Call there. Be here. Go there. Catch up, repair, take care. Take lots of care of your children. They need you. This is what being a parent is all about. It's a completely different thing from being just you. The "me, myself, and I" time is gone for now.

BASIC RULE NUMBER THREE: BE RESILIENT, NOT RIGID

Deal with it. At a certain point, as you are washed down the river of inevitable change, it is important to start rowing *with* the rushing of the water. Fighting the tide, rowing upstream, may get you nowhere but stuck in midstream. Facing spiraling societal and economic pressures, today's family has no choice but to a least subtly redefine itself—its purpose, its duration, its rules, its goals, its boundaries, the roles of each parent and child. When it cannot stay intact, relatively loyal to its original traditional form (which was typically the biologically defined two-parent family), then the family must and will undergo redefinition. No matter what its design, today's family must be resilient, adapting to pressures and new forms, to survive.

Both parents and children get lost in the shuffle. The directional instincts weaken and all too often shut down. You struggle to set your priorities. I mean, parents: This is your life. Or is it? You have arrived. Or have you? "Hey, at least you made it this far," they say, "don't look a gift horse in the mouth." Just drag yourself over the finish line and listen for a cheer. Or at least the sound of one hand clapping. After all, this parenting stuff is perhaps the greatest link between the divine and the downright hands-on, frontline, day-in-and-day-out, gritty, real life commitment you can make. Hard work? Yes. This is basic rule number three: bend or break, or at least be resilient, not rigid.

Think about it next time you're racing out to the all night drugstore for a prescription for your child at 11 at night, with your own fever of 102 degrees, hoping that the place also sells three ring binders because the other child absolutely has to take one into school tomorrow at 8 A.M. Or maybe you can think about it the next time you discover you are out of diapers after you have already started changing the baby's diapers just as the older one is throwing her tooth aligning retainer into the toilet because she cannot have five dollars right now and she saw this way of making a point on TV. And you thought you had unplugged the television set. And you hoped you had forgotten to pay its bill.

BASIC RULE NUMBER FOUR: LOVE BEING A PARENT

Oh, come on now, you love being a parent, and you know it. And it will always be a labor of love, from the very first leakproof baby diaper leaking all over your three-piece pinstriped suit to the first ticket your teenage driver gets when she or he backs into an army of parked Harleys at an all night coffee shop—a hundred miles away from home when you thought your child was at the local prom. These are your children. And, you know, you just know, deep in your heart, that you just have to love them. And you do, no doubt about it. As my own father used to say whenever I tried to thank him for all he had done for me, "Oh now, come on, what are fathers for?" I think he had it right. Why be a parent unless your commitment is to being one? (But then, how many people really think this through beforehand? I am told the answer is NONE!)

BASIC RULE NUMBER FIVE: BALANCE THINGS, JUST A BIT

But try to balance things just a bit—grab a little for yourself beyond the role of mom or dad or maybe even both at the same time if you are one of those "very very single parents" on your own and without much help. Do something for yourself once in a while. It'll help you stay alive. Save your life just a little bit. Your child will feel the effects. In fact, be just a little selfish once in a while. Get an hour's massage, or maybe just a fifteen minute one. Go away for a weekend, or maybe just for an hour. Cook your favorite food for dinner instead of everyone else's. Or don't cook. Run wild in small doses—maybe by reading three pages of a good book while taking a hot bath, getting your nails done, or eating a banana split.

Take a little for yourself. And really savor it while it lasts. This is a tough job—because when you let yourself take this little, you find you want a whole lot more, but it's just "a little" you can take. You have a moral responsibility to parent your offspring. This means that you are "on" about 200 percent of the time—no matter what you are doing, This is true in two-parent situations as well as in single-parent situations. If you are one of the growing army of single parents, single when it comes to the real stuff of parenting, the day in and day out commitment, the front line love, then you know who you are. You've been there, done that, got the T-shirt.

But, do try not to have your own identity crisis until those kids hit college. And I do mean hit. (I interviewed a woman who had disappeared for a week and come back married to a man twenty years younger than she—after her daughter drove the car into the wall of the college cafeteria by mistake. It was foggy and she thought it was a parking lot, the teen said.) In fact, try to wait until your children have raised their own children (your grandchildren). Otherwise your identity crisis can be confusing. You might switch roles or something. And you know how tempting this can be.

After all, this is the best of times, and this is the worst of times, for families today. Families are told that, if (IF) they can find a way to access them, there are so many options, so many opportunities, so many acceptable paths to follow. And so many decisions every step of the way. Single parents, married parents, stepparents, adopted parents, other parents, and their parents and their children, are living just about all the modern dilemmas on a day to day basis. Gender, relationship, child-rearing, aging, career, economic, and other major life questions are asked and answered continuously—almost automatically—often on the spur of the moment, because they have to be. There isn't time to deliberate while the dinner is burning, the bills need paying, the child is testing the limits, the water heater is broken, the neighbor's fifteen year old is pregnant, the other neighbors are driving drunk and so are their teenagers, and you have to find time to—(to what-oh you forget)—to live!

BASIC RULE NUMBER SIX: SEE THE BLESSINGS

It's a lot for parents. A sacred lot. A true blessing. Parenting is one of the most special paths that can be tread. I certainly wouldn't trade it away. Parents form families for children. (And yes, a single parent with one child also forms a family—the two of them are a unit too.) Families are the nests—the first origins—the starting point for the lives of the citizens of tomorrow, and for the caretakers of your generation when it retires into tomorrow. Parents, think of the times you are up all night with a sick child, there for your child no matter what, flashing on your own old age and wondering who will be there for you? Or maybe trying not to ask yourself this question, trying not to see these pictures.

So you plug right in and do just what you are supposed to do: you raise your child and send your child to school. Day in and day out you see your child grow and engage in some way with the world outside the home. You obediently (and even gladly quite often) surrender your child into the arms of the educational system, the child-care, training, and employment control function society calls "K through 12," on a regular basis. And this is what you are supposed to do. So you're doing the right thing, you tell yourself on the occasions when you begin to question even yourself (especially perhaps when your child comes home and says that her high school looks like the inside of a toilet and you visit the school and sort of see why when you walk the halls during recess. And you wonder how those teachers handle all this young energy, these colorful members of this adolescent generation testing the limits, testing authority, testing the truth, as they should be. But should they be spray painting the school hallways?)

You wave goodbye as your offspring unit (your child) rushes off into the future citizen production line (your child's school) for just another day of education. Those poor teachers, spelling the parents so they can perform their other societal functions while inducing learning in the parents' offspring. How good of these teachers. What an underpaid service to us all. Educators work hard. They deal with many of the issues parents do, on a broader scale, many times a day. While some high schools struggle to set policy regarding students' breastfeeding of their newborn babies in class, others are focusing more on gun control. And gum control. A teacher told me the other day that her students played a terrible joke on her, and left a lot of "a.b.c. gum" (already been chewed gum) on her chair. She sat in it before she knew it was there. Still, she said, this is better than kids coming to class with loaded guns.

BASIC RULE NUMBER SEVEN: WATCH FOR THE HIGHER PURPOSE

And then they come home again, in need of parental contact, and in need of fighting it, needing to be close to the very persons they need to rebel against in order to define themselves and forge an identity. This double bind is normal, even healthy. But it's a lot for a parent, especially while you work continuously trying to hold a job, stay barely healthy enough to run the show, and see the light. Light? Yes, the higher purpose to this all. It helps to find a higher purpose, if you have a second or two to reflect, maybe at a red light or while you clean the ceiling after your nine year old tried to boil eggs and forgot about them on high, until the water boiled away, and the eggs, left to cook another hour or more, exploded upward.

Maybe you are one of those people in one of those two-career marriages. You have a teenager who is entirely uninterested in babysitting the two year old you also have, and who seems to have decided that she or he is an adult and should report in only occasionally and use your house as a hotel. You might have parents in their eighties who are too infirm to help with your two year old and have no rapport with your thirteen year old and who wish they could live with you even though your house—and your poor overcrowded taxed to the max life—is too small. Maybe you are one of those who is usually too tense or too tired to have fun with your spouse—if you have one at all any more. And maybe whenever you manage to find a babysitter in order to go out, you are just too tired to do so.

BASIC RULE NUMBER EIGHT: SEE THE
GRACE IN THE PAIN

You have to see the grace in the pain. I am reminded of a woman I knew who was dying of cancer while her child was still of preschool age. She laid on the floor, so thin her body was reduced to a collection of bones, and told me that she thought she should die soon, but that she wanted to stay alive as long as she could in any way harvest the joy of watching her child grow so very much as each second passed. She had seen and had cherished the finest of the most minute moments of her child's existence, and of the relationship between them. Her daughter came running in at that very moment, with some baby clothes. She wanted to put these on her mother, advising her mother that she was "growing down" so quickly that now they could put these old clothes to good use. They didn't really fit, but the act of laying the clothes on her mother's body seemed to satisfy the little girl. It was the love in the act of this daughterly dressing that made me smile.

You know, life has its large and its small pains. It helps to see grace in every second. Sometimes we have to look hard for the grace, but to want to look for the grace is already a start.

BASIC RULE NUMBER NINE: FIND HUMOR IN EVEN
THE MOST DIFFICULT

Here's a funny story. Really, it is rather funny, if you follow it through to the end. I tell this story because sometimes there is humor in troubling situations, and laughing a bit can help. And this was surely a troubling situation.

I couldn't help but remember my mother's preparation for her own funeral as she died of cancer. I was seventeen, and she was forty-three. She was quite aware she would not be around as I moved into adulthood, had my own babies, experienced the joys and challenges of child-rearing. Time was limited, and our interactions measured. We knew that each and every thing we did and said would be pretty much the last we would share.

I wasn't surprised when my mother engaged me a conversation about what she would wear in her open casket. She had excellent taste. She chose a navy blue suit to look dignified, classically elegant, and respectful of the occasion. Being a typical teenage girl, she and I had a slight disagreement regarding the importance of gloves, white gloves, as usual. She wanted me to wear them too. But, I told her I wanted to feel the air on my hands and not feel them encased in some claustrophobic hand mask. She said that handglove-induced claustrophobia wasn't something she would feel if she wore gloves in her casket, but then she had never minded wearing gloves anyway. I told her that this was a silly conversation and that I would never forget its absurdity. She said that this was good, that she would "always remember it this way." And that maybe now I would "always remember your gloves, or at least what they symbolize."

Sure enough, my mother found a way to embed a loving and living riddle I will never forget into that fleeting moment. After all, what are mothers for? I tell this story to remind everyone to laugh a little—too see humor in whatever you can see it in. Just a little humor, enough to make you smile just a little. Smiling helps immensely.

BASIC RULE NUMBER TEN: CHERISH THE MOMENTS

Parents, when you think you are wearing out, that it is all for naught, that you may not make it another day, stop. Look deep inside, at the very heart of the nitty-gritty, real life moments you share with your children. Rethink your idea of quality time. It's all quality time, if you give it quality. Love is what happens in those moments when the preciousness of life hits you full on. It is there, on this microscopic day in and day out level that the real transactions between you are made. Sure, you cannot do it all according to a recipe. Things are rarely perfect. It's not all smiles and kisses. But you can do it. In a world hungry for the sacred, starving for the light, parents touch it every day.

And knowing this can help us as we try to raise thinking children and teens, and as we try to help maximize their mental and moral potentials. After all, what are we parents for but to touch the future through our children? Why would we be parents if not to have an effect on the world through our offspring?

Does $-5^2 = (-5)^2$?

No, they equal two different things. $-5^2 = -25$ and $(-5)^2 = 25$.

1) Translate: $-x^2$ and $(-x)^2$ into words.
$-x^2 =$ square X and take the opposite or negative of it.
$(-x)^2 =$ take the opposite of X, then square it.

2) Is $-x^2$ the same as $(-x^2)$?
No, they're opposites. One has a positive value and the other has a negative value.

3) Evaluate $-x^2$ for $x = 2, 0, -1, -3 \rightarrow -4, 0, -1, -9$
$(-x)^2$ for $x = 2, 0, -1, -3 \rightarrow 4, 0, 1, 9$

Homework

=47 To squared numbers produce parabolic graphs, and a number times another number produce line graphs

=48 ⓐ Both graphs have 12.56, both start at zero, Graph #1 is linear, #2 is curve
ⓑ Graph #1 would be 16, #2 would be 18
ⓒ 10 would be 120
ⓓ 20 would be approx. 1256

=49 ⓐ 13 ⓑ

X	1	2	3	4	5	6	7	8	9	10
Y	1	5	9	13	17	21	25	29	33	37

$4x - 3 = Y$

=50

length $3x$	width X	area $3x^2$	Check 18.75
3	1	12	L
9	3	27	H
7.5	2.5	18.75	✓

=51 ⓐ $y = x^2 - 3 =$ parabola because it's squared
ⓑ $y = 2x - 3 =$ linear graph because it's multiplied by 2

=53 ⓐ $5 \cdot 4 - 3 \cdot (2 - 3^2)$ $3 - 7$ ⓑ $3(12 + 8.6 - 2 - 5)$
$20 - 21 = -41$ $3(12 + 12.2 - 5)$
$3 \cdot 24.2 = 72.6$

Modern Education and Intelligence (Illustration by Evacheska deAngelis)

Part One

Moral Intelligence and
Mental Ability

CHAPTER 2

How Moral Intelligence Is Relevant to Learning and Living

We sail a changing sea
through halcyon days and storm,
Our compass trembles in the binnacle ...
and wisdom lies in the masterful administration
of the unforeseen.

Robert Bridges, "Testament of Beauty"

We cannot even begin to estimate the massive importance of parents' and teachers' roles in raising thinking children and teens (both of which I tend to call "children" herein, as they are all our children regardless of their ages). Basically, the roles and behaviors of parents and teachers have powerful effects on the outcomes of growing up and of going to school while growing up. In fact, many of the chapters in this book discuss what parents and teachers can think about as they work to raise and educate thinking children and teens. However, before proceeding with these chapters, I insert this chapter on moral intelligence. This is because all the mental ability in the world cannot guarantee its wise use.

This is why we want to aim for a high level of development in the area of moral intelligence, a type of intelligence that has not been explored as much as other areas of intelligence, despite the fact that it is one of the most important areas. Moral intelligence helps us make good decisions, decisions that are well thought out, and also helps us know how to think about what we are being told by others are good decisions. Moral intelligence helps us know for ourselves what we actually think about an issue, an event, a situation, a problem. Our children and teens have a right to begin developing their own moral intelligences at an early age and then throughout their childhoods, and they need us to guide them in this development.

WISE AND RIGHT USE OF MENTAL ABILITY

Now, of course the wise and right use of mental ability does vary according to one's own world view, belief system, and other value systems. And this variation is a good thing, as it allows for diversity of world views. Still, there are some very basic and very universal aspects, core characteristics, of moral sensitivity and moral intelligence regardless of personal, family, and cultural choices as to belief system and religious orientation. Hence, these few words here before proceeding to the following chapters are words about what is perhaps most important of everything discussed in this book—*moral intelligence*—the ability of a young person, or of anyone of any age, to make good, even wise, decisions, and to know how to do so, when to do so, and what it looks like when others are doing so (or not doing so). This moral intelligence ability can be expressed in concert with one's own or one's family belief system, or it may reach beyond to broader, more universal themes. (Of course these may be one in the same.)

WHAT IS MORAL INTELLIGENCE?

By moral intelligence I do not mean morality itself. Morality is a complex issue best reserved for another book. Here I just want to remark that much of what we call morality is actually what we have been taught that good is. Of course it is good that we learn about what good is, and what it means to do the right thing. And while social guidance (such as laws, religion, culture, family, and even tradition) can certainly help guide us in doing what is right and what is best and what is good, there is a fundamental difference between this *social guidance* and what I call *moral intelligence* itself. Although they do influence each other a great deal, social guidance comes from outside ourselves, and personal moral intelligence come from within.

Our own personal moral intelligence is needed when we must decide something for ourselves—decide on an action or form an opinion on our own, sometimes in addition to, and sometimes independently of, law, religion, tradition, and teaching coming to us from outside ourselves. Even a young person needs a personal moral intelligence. Personal moral intelligence is necessary in many different situations. We see this need so often when young people are invited or pressured (by their peers or by television commercials, for example) to do things that are not necessarily the right or best or good things for them to do at their age or perhaps at any age.

Think of the common instance where a teen does not know what to do when pressured to play a game at a party, perhaps a simple one such as spin the bottle, a kissing game. Or think of another common instance when a young person is pressured to smoke a cigarette. There are many reasons why that young person may not be able to draw on teaching coming from outside her- or himself to respond to this pressure. In fact, even adults may find themselves in similar situations from time to time. These situations take place, for example,

- when we do not have a relevant teaching coming from outside ourselves to call upon or,
- when we do not understand how the teaching coming from outside ourselves applies to a particular situation or issue or,
- when we sense that perhaps the teaching coming from outside ourselves may not be being interpreted correctly or appropriately for a particular situation or issue or,
- when events lead us to question the teaching coming from outside ourselves, leaving us only with what we have inside to guide us or,
- when there is not teaching coming from outside ourselves, or we do not see that there is this teaching.

It is in these instances that we need our own internal compasses, our own personal moral intelligences to guide us. And it is in the above instances that our children and teens need to know what it means to have and to access their own moral intelligences, and when and how to use the reasoning and thinking processes that operate their own moral intelligences.

DECISION MAKING IS CENTRAL

Decision making is central to the application of moral intelligence in daily life. Decision making is something we all constantly engage in, whether or not we realize we are doing so. So many minor decisions are being made at all times, that we have to make some of these on the semi-conscious and even automatic level just to be able to go about our daily activities. For example, waving a fly away when we are in a hurry to write an urgent note, or turning on the windshield wipers when driving through a sudden rain shower, are decisions we may make almost automatically for good reason; however, these are still decisions we have made. And then there are the bigger decisions, such as what to do when someone says something cruel to you, or when you need to get a job (or a piece of homework) done on time and put other important activities aside in order to do it. And then there are the sort of decisions made without much if any conscious thinking, on the spur of the moment, or on impulse, when these would have been better made after thinking through a decision-making process.

Many decisions require placing importance—value—on a choice, and comparing the choices or options available so as to choose from among these. Should I go this way or that way? Should I spend my money on this or on that? Should I respond to this insult this way or that way? Should I say yes to this opportunity or that one? Should I say yes or no? Should I believe my parents when they say this is dangerous or should I not? Should I care whether this is dangerous or should I not? Will this be dangerous if I do it just this one time? How dangerous is this? And so on. Clearly, decision making involves making choices, choices to or not to. Making a good choice is making a good decision.

MAKING A GOOD DECISION IS A PROCESS

What is a good decision? Good can mean different things to different people. The meaning of good varies. So let's focus on *decision* instead of on *good* here. We can focus on this word—decision, and so can our children—just as soon as they can recognize these two words, good and decision, that is. There is perhaps no age too young to begin hearing the word decision and to begin seeing adults working to make good decisions. This is a behavior that can be learned.

What goes into a good decision? A good decision-making *process*! We can help our children and teens learn this once we understand it for ourselves. What is a good decision-making process? This is a series of steps that lead to a clear and logical and yes, morally intelligent, decision. So often we do not emphasize for ourselves, let alone for our children, what goes into a good decision-making process. Although making good decisions is a noble concept, and a fine goal, really making good decisions involves the process itself. Adults and children can learn to look for the process and the quality of the process of decision making, not just for the decision itself.

Too often, in our personal let alone work lives, we place all the emphasis on the decision and fail to look at how the decision was made. We can change this behavior in the next generation if not also in our own generation, by making the process of making the decision most important. We can learn a great deal about the importance of the process itself by watching political processes in democratic countries. For example, we do quite rightly care about the outcome of presidential elections, and yet, perhaps even more so, we care about the process by which we arrive at this outcome. In the United States, we emphasize the importance of the process of electing a president. We and our children can learn to take the high value we place on this national process down to the personal level.

After all, a good decision is one that is arrived at through a good decision-making process. So we want to place value (for ourselves and for our children) on the process used to arrive at a decision. Returning to what I said earlier, so many decisions are made without thinking, and often it is after the fact that we wish we had thought before deciding. The old saying, "Think before you act," is great advice. We have all heard it many times. Now, let's take this to the next level, and let's *think about thinking* before we act. What does this thinking look like? Have we thought this decision through enough? What does this process of making a decision to (or not to) take an action look like? The process of thinking through a decision is the key here.

DECISION MAKING AND PROBLEM SOLVING: THE *HOW* MATTERS HERE

Decision making is a form of problem solving. We believe in teaching our children what it means to solve math and other schoolwork problems (something we go into later in this book). Now, let's also believe in teaching our children to make good decisions by engaging in good decision-making processes. We certainly can teach young people what it means to make a good decision, how to make a good decision. We must understand for ourselves what this is so that we can teach this to our young people.

Again, decision making is a form of problem solving. The problem is: what is the right answer? The solving is: the process of getting the answer, the decision-making process of arriving at the right answer. Later in this book, I delve into the problem-solving process itself as it relates to school work, for example. Both the general decision-making process I describe in this chapter and the schoolwork type of problem-solving process I describe later involve thinking about thinking. Both processes require us to stop, to slow down, to see ourselves think through the decision-making (or problem-solving) process. It is in this slowing down to hear ourselves think, to think about *how* we are thinking about the decision or problem, that we gain a great deal of control over our minds. And this is intelligence at work, our own intelligence.

DECISION-MAKING QUESTIONS

As parents and teachers, we must know this to teach this: When we take the time to consciously think through questions such as these listed below, we are no longer making decisions without thinking things through. Now we own our decision-making processes. We own the process of asking ourselves and answering for ourselves questions such as these:

The What, When, Who of Decision-Making

What: WHAT IS THE DECISION I (OR WE) NEED TO MAKE?

When: HOW MUCH TIME DO I (OR WE) HAVE TO MAKE THIS DECISION?

Who: WHO IS MAKING THIS DECISION?

But Who: WHO *SHOULD* BE MAKING THIS DECISION?

The Know What, Know More, Know Where

Know What: What do I know that will help me make this decision?

Know More: Do I need to know more to make this decision?

Know Where: Where can I find out more if I need to know more?

The Consequences

Who Benefits: Who benefits if I say yes, if I say no, if I say nothing right now?

Who Benefits When: When do the benefits take place? Now? Later?

What Good: What is the greatest good that can be done here?

What Outcomes: What are the consequences?

What Harm: Is anyone harmed? Who?

What Risk: What are the dangers or risks?

What Value: How do the benefits compare to the risks?

The Am I Ready

Am I Ready: Am I ready and able to make this decision right now?

LEAD BY EXAMPLE

I cannot stress enough how important it is for parents and teachers to know what they are talking about when they tell children and teens what to do. There is no use asking young people to make good decisions and to think before acting if we adults do not model this. It is important to lead by example when teaching decision making to children, not only to young children but also to children and teens of any age.

Even when your child is fully grown, she or he may still be easily influenced and act based on the decisions others make for your child or urge your child to make. We need to learn, and we are always learning, how to make good decisions for ourselves. The process is life-long. We must focus on the reality that young people learn moral intelligence most easily by viewing a strong example of moral intelligence at work, one in a parent or a sibling (ideally in both and in all persons around the child or teen). Children must see and hear older persons such as parents in the process of making decisions. Watching people think for themselves, seeing what goes into thinking for oneself, children learn to value the process of thinking for oneself when making decisions.

TEACHING YOUNG PEOPLE TO THINK FOR THEMSELVES

Although I emphasize leading by example, revealing to young people the process of one's decision making, it is also important to encourage your children to think for themselves, to practice what they see adults doing when they are making good, well thought out decisions. Seeing your child make a good decision on her or his own will be even more gratifying when you realize that your previous examples taught the child (or teen) how to fend for her- or himself when a tough decision had to be made and you were not around to give assistance.

Teaching young people to think on their own is done through the tools you give them, and model for them, beginning even before they have to think on their own. Parents, with care and attention to the process, you can equip your children with what they will need when they will have to think on their own. You can also equip your children with the understanding that they are learning tools to use when thinking on their own—and when thinking in general! They are thinking *about* their thinking processes, their decision-making processes!

WITH MATURITY CAN COME BETTER DECISION-MAKING PROCESSES

Young children tend to make most of their decisions based on how these will affect them and only them right now. As they grow, young people (hopefully) make decisions based not only on how the outcome will affect them personally but also on how it will affect others now and in the future. This growing concern for more than just self plays an ever-increasing role in decision making. Moral intelligence increases as the outcomes of decisions are understood to affect more than just the self, and more than just the now.

Good judgment is an ability that develops as young people grow up, an ability that never stops developing. We like to think that we make better and better decisions as we age. Whether or not this is true, what we should be emphasizing is that the process of making these decisions becomes more and more intelligent. We learn to be morally intelligent—and then more and more morally intelligent.

THE FOUR R'S: RESPECT, RESPONSIBILITY, REASON, AND REALITY

We can teach our children the four basic rules of decision making: respect, responsibility, reason, and reality:

- *Respect oneself and others* when working to think through a decision. We want to make a decision that is good for ourselves, yes, but one that is actually good for others as well. We want to do no harm.
- *Be responsible* for the decision you are making. Think about what will happen once you make this decision.
- *Reason through* your decision. Think about all the questions you must ask before making this decision. Do not make a decision without the proper information. Go through the steps involved in thinking this decision through to the end.
- *See reality* when making your decision. What you do is taking place in the world around you. Realize where you are in place and time and culture. See the environment in which you are making your decision.

THE GREATER GOOD

This highest value we can place on a decision-making process is the greater good value. We can ask ourselves, no matter how old we are: How many people benefit from this decision and is this something I am thinking about as I decide?

Here moral intelligence can filter into all we do and all we learn and all we think. Moral intelligence is an ability that can be learned, practiced, developed. This is the human ability we are so much in need of as we move into the future. Our young people can learn moral intelligence, learn how to develop this intelligence, learn how to apply this intelligence in all they do. They can take this form of intelligence to a new level. Let's keep this in mind as we work through the discussions in this book, the tools for raising thinking children and teens. We must keep in mind at all times: All the mental ability in the world is of no great use without a strong moral intelligence to guide its use.

CHAPTER 3

Introduction to Human Potential

Knowledge is power.

Sir Francis Bacon, *Religious Meditations: Of Heresies*

At last they heard the sound of slow shuffling footsteps approaching the door from the inside. It seemed, as the Mole remarked to the Rat, like someone walking in carpet slippers that were too large for him and down-at-the-heel; which was intelligent of Mole, because that was exactly what he was.

Kenneth Grahame, *The Wind in the Willows*

Intelligence is many things, many abilities. We tend to think of intelligence as being primarily academic intelligence. We also tend to have opinions about who is more intelligent and who is less intelligent. But do these opinions work for us? Do they help us use the wealth of ability we have among all of us?

There are questions we must dare to ask. What is intelligence? Are we stuck with the level of intelligence with which we are born? If not, if one's intelligence level is determined after birth, then can we raise intelligence during childhood and adolescence? Can parents raise their children's and their teen's intelligence? In fact, we might also ask whether parents, all adults, can raise their own intelligences and reasoning processes?

After all, in guiding young people it is helpful to see for ourselves the path—or at least its starting point. And, can adults walk the path of growing mental ability with their children? Can parents perhaps raise their own intelligences while working to guide their children and teens in discovering the true potential of their minds?

And what does it mean to think? Can we actually think independently? Can we actually think for ourselves? What does this mean to us? And can we actually teach our children and teens to think independently? **Can we actually teach them to think?** As science tells us more and more about the neurological activities of the brain, about lengths of brain reaction time to new information, and about time involved in processing that information, we can work to help young people maximize the precious moments of brain time and development as these speed by.

Parents, teachers-educators, and policy makers can set forth an attitude that: promotes mental and moral development in young people of all ages; suggests ways to think about intelligence; and, describes methods of raising mental abilities and intellectual performances. Tall order? Well, perhaps it is. The starting point, however, is simply knowing that children *can* be taught *how* to concentrate. They can also be taught how to think, how to learn, how to organize their thoughts, how to make decisions, and, ultimately, how to be intelligent. Adults can create an atmosphere that fosters the expression of intelligence and encourages attitudes that place value on intelligent, creative, and independent thinking.

CREATING A REALITY IN WHICH MINDS FLOURISH

Parents and teachers can create a reality in which children's minds flourish—*all* children's minds. To create this reality, we must all develop our understandings of both mental and moral ability. We must all examine our assumptions regarding intelligence, our views of our own and our children's abilities and thought processes. We need not settle for the notion that ability levels are set in stone and that is that. And yet we often do settle for this notion, even when we do not see ourselves doing so. Instead, we can choose to see the unlimited potential within each of us and within each of our children. Unlimited potential is sleeping—dormant—until awakened.

Schools as well as parents can look more closely at the effect of educational labeling, tracking, and even the sometimes incorrect or biased identification of some children as "gifted children" and others as "not gifted." How dangerous incorrect labeling can be! And yet how ready we are to allow this labeling to take place, even the invisible labeling taking place in our own minds. Yes, we do label ourselves and our children simply by not seeing the unlimited potential there. And if we do this subtle labeling even without realizing it, just see how much labeling our social and educational systems are doing all the time, some of this quite harmful, even dangerous.

NEGLECTING A CHILD'S MIND IS NEGLECT

Some places (such as some schools, not all, of course) where we may leave our children to be labeled and tracked into learning levels and opportunities can indeed be harmful, even dangerous. We do need to keep a watchful eye on this. Of course we want to know as much as we can about our children's schools (of course, yes?). We have a right to know (and our children have a right to have us know) what to look for when making judgments about our preschools (where children are under kindergarten age) and schools (where children are K-12 age). And, certainly, we know that we have rights to know about possible neglect and abuse, yes? Some of us even make special notes on possible signs of neglect and possible indications of forms of abuse in some of these settings.

I refer to neglect and abuse here, not because they are center stage here in this book, but because there are many forms of neglect and abuse that are not seen as such. I want to make it clear that *neglecting a child's potential is neglect. And abusing a child's potential is abuse.*

Whatever role we play in children's lives, our involvement in their educations—the encouraging of their mental and moral abilities—can either cultivate and or squelch this great and irreplaceable national resource: the mind of the next generation. It is our responsibility as parents, educators, policy makers, and taxpayers to empower the young to develop their intelligences, to teach them to think for themselves, and to prepare them for a future that we can only imagine. In educating children, we are building not only the adults of tomorrow but also the future of the world. Indeed, a mind is a terrible thing to waste. And so is the future.

EMPOWERING YOUNG PEOPLE

Empowering young people, the next generation, our children and teens, to thrive in an uncertain, unpredictable, future is challenging. What can we give our precious offspring to help them grow into a future world (a future work force, future state of technology, future economy, future society, future environment) as yet undefined? What is it we can do to prepare them for now, and for decades from now? We need to see that we *can* guide our children and teens in a way that they can later transfer the abilities to learn and make good decisions to their own children and teens, and thereby to the generations which follow. Such a profound responsibility it is to raise children and teens, let alone thinking children and teens!

You may have heard it said that "thinking is overrated," and that "ignorance is bliss." This is perhaps indicative of the tendency we have to confuse what is not really thinking with what is really thinking. Sloppy thinking and failure to really think are acts of not thinking. These are not acts of thinking well and thinking clearly. Good thinking, real thinking, can never be overrated—except when we do not recognize the difference between not thinking well and not thinking at all and really thinking. It is essential that parents recognize the difference between not thinking clearly and not thinking well and really thinking. Parents, the teachers who work with their children and teens, and the policy makers who fund (and do not fund) educational programs and services must model this difference. This means that parents themselves must understand the difference between not thinking and thinking. In this sense, this book is about all of us, and contains suggestions for how we guide the mental and moral development not only of our children and teens but also of ourselves as adults, as models, and as individuals who know something about the abilities we want to instill in our children.

Again, this book is about guiding the mental and moral development of children and teens. I refer to children and teens throughout this book; however there are times when I call this group "young people" and times when I call them all "children." After all, your child, whether one-year-old or eighteen, is still your child and still a young person. The information contained in this book can be valuable no matter what age your child.

For example, ideas about raising an eight-year-old are important information when raising a fourteen-year-old. And, ideas about raising a sixteen-year-old are important information when raising a six-year-old. Yes, of course parenting must be age appropriate; however, parenting must also reflect an understanding of what pieces of development are coming as the child grows, or may need to be reemphasized in later childhood and adolescence. For example, know that, as a child grows, the influence of outside factors, including friends and nonfamily members, increases. Parents should begin talking about making good decisions very early. Do this so that once parents' influence is not the main influence in a child's life, what it means to make good decisions is already deeply instilled in that child's (yes, and teen's) mind. Another example, finding a teen struggling to organize school and life demands may indicate that essential development of organizational skills is weak and may need support. Because development at all ages reflects development at all other ages, I suggest even parents of older children and teens read through all these chapters, including the all-important very basic material on organization.

Even where I herein refer to particular age groups, the information may be useful no matter what age your child or teen. In fact, I have given this material to teens and young adults to read. They then review their own stages in the development of their own thinking and decision-making skills. Just knowing what goes into building thinking skills helps many children and teens (and their parents) become aware of thinking itself. This is because the development of the mind, while coming in stages, also takes place continuously (yes, even at your age, if you, the reader, are an adult). Anything you feel you may have missed, you can still bring to your own mental development and also to your parenting and or teaching of young people. You can find ways to adapt this material—or at least sensitize yourself to this material—no matter what the current age of your child or teen. Where you may not have had the opportunity before now to do something I suggest herein with your child or teen (again, they are all children), you may be able to come up with your own version of it now. In fact, just being aware of what activities and steps in thinking through things contribute to the ability of the mind to reason and to make decisions—to think well, can have a most positive effect.

THINKING IS ITS OWN INTELLIGENCE

So often we hear it said that someone is "smarter" or "more intelligent" than someone else. And so often this is incorrect. Instead it may be that some are able to think well while others are not yet able to think well, or are not able to think well in particular circumstances such as during tests or during interactions with certain friends. So essential to the functioning of the mind is thinking that we must step back from assessments of intelligence itself to see where thinking well and thinking clearly are central to being intelligent. Engaging young people of all ages (and yourself) in *thinking about thinking* can raise the ability of the mind and the person with the mind to think. In fact, you can start this discussion very early, as early as you want. (On this note, I thank my own daughter for allowing me to teach her, at an early age, about what it means to *think about thinking*, and about what it means to engage in what I call *conscious metacognition*, conscious operating of mental functions. I discuss metacognition later in this book.)

THINKING AND INTELLIGENCE

We want to get to thinking itself. But let's go back to this thing we call "intelligence." Then we can ask whether the two, thinking and intelligence, are truly related. Then we can really talk about what it takes to raise thinking children and teens, young people who think intelligently. So, here again come questions we must ask: What is intelligence? Is it a gift or something that one works very hard to develop? If intelligence is a gift, how does one get it? Is one born with it or does some wonderful schoolteacher come along and plant it or grow it in one's mind? Are we stuck with the level of intelligence with which we are born? If not, if one's intelligence level is determined after birth, then can we raise intelligence during childhood? Can parents raise their children's intelligence?

These are good questions. Researchers offer a variety of definitions of intelligence, many of them conflicting; therefore, knowing what intelligence actually is is the challenge. Definitions of intelligence range from biological definitions (which say that intelligence in biologically determined and affected), to environmental definitions (which say that intelligence is determined by the environment, the world surrounding the individual) to what are today the most common combinations of these definitions. Definitions include "single" intelligences and "multiple" intelligences. They even include newer definitions of intelligence such as musical, artistic, emotional and leadership intelligences. Of course, I must say here that a newly defined intelligence may have existed long before that intelligence is identified as an intelligence. There are forms of intelligence we are just now recognizing, just now seeing, as we are finding we need them in our new and ever-changing world. On the other hand, we are also actually generating new intelligences as the world changes. For example, technical programming intelligence is an area that, while involving age-old forms of logic, can be said to be a new intelligence. Another emerging intelligence may be the ability to use brain signals to operate complex equipment such as fighter jets—to, in essence, do this just by thinking.

CONTROVERSY OVER AND EXPANSION OF INTELLIGENCE

There has been a great deal of scientific, social, and political controversy over the theory that intelligence is biologically determined. Although I find this debate limiting, I think it is important to understand it. Therefore, this discussion is included at the start of this book. If intelligence were entirely genetic, inherited, you might have no opportunity to change your intelligence level or that of your child's. This would say that intelligence levels are set in stone, or better speaking, in genes. Some theorists have claimed that there is a core intelligence, a single "I.Q.," an intelligence factor or "intelligence quotient," and that this is inherited. Others have claimed that society labels some children as more intelligent, but that this is a sociopolitical artifact and not at all biologically determined. In the latter view, academic and other mental achievement is in no way predetermined at birth. This view says that environmental opportunities and stimulation determine intelligence and achievement in the world. This view says that the "better" the environment in which a child is reared, the "better" the child's mind will function and the "better" the child will perform. Certainly this view gives us hope that we can make a difference in the outcome of young people's (and even our own) mental development. I say that there are great opportunities for raising the mental ability of our population as a whole, of each of us alone plus all of us together. I also say that we must recognize these opportunities and make full use of them. I take this view and expand on it throughout this book. I insist that with more attention to thinking itself, we can empower everyone to develop various intelligences. Certainly critical thinking classes are a start. However, much more along the lines of thinking about thinking itself can be added to the standard critical thinking curriculum. The opportunities are unlimited. **There is no ceiling on mental development.**

Returning to the argument that intelligence is biologically based, or at least largely biologically influenced, note that biology here is not restricted to genetics. What this means is that environmental factors such as nutrition and diet can have a great influence on mental functioning. What this also means is that intelligence is not predetermined, that there is much that can be done to enhance a person's (yes, yours, your child's, your teen's, your parents' too) intelligence during a lifetime, and especially during developmental years.

WORK WITH THE HARDWARE

Some biological theories of intelligence focus not on genetic inheritance, but more on the notion of "mental hardware": the neural connections in the brain. These are the places where the brain matter and nervous systems form links or connections to facilitate the brain's thinking and information storage. I want to note here that retaining what is learned is an important part of thinking. My view is that when the mind thinks about thinking quite consciously, what can be stored in the mental hardware is not only what is learned or at least remembered but also the thought processes themselves: These are the thoughts that have worked with the information.

In other words, the mind's memory function can store not only facts, and not only invisible, unconscious, automatic thought processes, but also conscious, purposeful thought processes. Recall how the smell of a special meal or favorite food can be remembered from childhood. Just think how much purposeful thinking about thinking might also be remembered from childhood. In fact, children who have been exposed to critical thinking courses frequently later (years later, even as adults) report the increasing value of that early training as they age. My view is that critical thinking can consciously work with mental hardware: the neural connections formed by conscious thinking about thinking add a whole network of ability to whatever else is learned or at least stored in the brain. This is because an added layer, more like an added network of neural connections, has been formed. Parents and teachers who are conscious of this potential, the potential for this added neural networking, can encourage its development every step of the way. Much as mathematicians and musicians appear to develop complex areas of the brain related to their specialties, we can envision areas of the brain related to thinking about thinking being enhanced.

BRAIN SIGNALS

Brain science has brought us many fascinating theories of brain function such as theories of signal transmission—theories of speed, intensity, and duration of electrical pulses across the brain. Certain studies are concluding that the speed of this signal transmission across the brain is related to measurable mental ability. Whether the efficiency of the brain's signal transmission is biologically inherited or developed as a result of environmental stimulation is also subject to ongoing debate, although these days the debate is far more complex. Most child development experts and neuroscientists agree that the eventual adult-level efficiency of signal transmission across the brain is highly influenced by the environment, especially during early childhood, when the brain is developing most rapidly. If this is the case, then parents who start early may have a great deal of influence over their children's intelligence, including the speed at which they think, their memory capacities, their specific abilities, and their concentration levels. (Parents who start later can still have a powerful effect on their children's and teens' intelligence.) This says a great deal about the influence of environmental stimulation on mental ability and the expression of mental development.

Back to brain speed. What about the basic issue of brain speed? Is thinking faster actually thinking better? Not necessarily; however, this is not the central issue right here. What is relevant here is that speedy signal transmission across the brain may make it possible for more connections to be made between old information already stored in the brain and fresh incoming information. The more connections that are made, the more useful new information is and the greater the likelihood that it will be used in one or more ways; and then remembered (and stored in the brain) in one or more ways; and then accessed when needed in one or more ways. Speedy transmission may therefore also improve information storage and information access—memory capability.

Memory itself is certainly another area that seems to be related to intelligence. However, memory is a complex and varied thing. A person with a photographic memory may or may not be intelligent. Remembering every word on a page but not being able to think about these words is merely storing information well and not using it.

INTELLIGENCE AS IT WAS ONCE DEFINED MAY NOT EXIST

The concept of "intelligence" itself may be outdated; in some ways it is an old-fashioned concept. Perhaps we should speak instead of various mental abilities. Perhaps we best refer to intelligences plural and the various mental abilities these represent every time we talk about intelligence these days. However, whether or not the word "intelligence" is used is less important than the idea that there are, indeed, varying degrees of mental competence in many different areas, some of which we may not have yet discovered. A high level of mathematical ability and a high level of verbal ability are not always found together. Verbal, mathematical, musical, artistic, spatial, leadership, planning, and other mental abilities are, according to some definitions of intelligence, specific and very separate intelligences. A person may be "good" in some of these areas and not others. The difference in favored abilities is the result of a range of factors, and there is no single explanation.

CONCENTRATION

Whatever the specific area of intelligence or mental ability, that area can be enhanced by concentration. Concentration is critical in mental development. Parents of school children seem to know this when they ask whether or not their children can be taught to concentrate. The ability to concentrate appears to be powerfully influenced by environment. And, because concentration affects mental ability, the environment that influences concentration also influences mental ability.

Let's concentrate on concentration for a moment. Most people, children as well as adults, have down times, or times when they are less able to focus on particular mental tasks. Sometimes, but quite rarely, organic brain disorders disrupt concentration. However, the inability to concentrate is usually related to a variety of more simple and remediable conditions, including but not limited to lack of interest in the subject, fatigue due to inadequate sleep and diet, distractions such as noise, and personal and family emotional problems. And, often, children (and their parents) just do not know how to concentrate. Most of us have not had the benefit of any form of direct concentration training. If concentration empowers thinking and if concentration can be taught, we have at least one way to enhance our children's mental development: emphasize, place great value on, teach and model the suggestion:

Concentrate.

Concentrate.

Concentrate.

Concentrate to think clearly and well.

CREATING AN INTELLIGENCE-ENHANCING REALITY

In this book, I am offering parents, teachers, policy makers, and anyone interested in thinking well an attitude that promotes mental development in young people (and for that matter in anyone of any age who cares to apply the conscious-thinking approaches presented herein to her- or himself). I am suggesting ways to think about intelligence and methods for raising young people's (and their parents') mental ability and intellectual performance. Children and teens can indeed be taught how to concentrate. They can also be taught how to think, how to organize their thoughts, how to learn, and, ultimately, they can be taught how to be intelligent. An atmosphere that fosters the expression of intelligence can be provided. Parents and educators can hold attitudes that value the steps involved in, and the actual nature of, intelligent and creative thinking. **We can place great value on actual thinking itself.** The essence of my message is that adults, parents and teachers, can create a reality in which children's minds flourish, and thereby create a reality in which their own minds flourish as well. To create this reality, we must all develop our understandings of mental ability.

As a parent, you have a responsibility to your child: You are responsible for a great deal of that child's development. Mental development begins at home, at birth, and, most likely, even in the womb. And it never stops. Don't overlook the opportunity to actualize your child's potential. Your own child's mind is perhaps your most precious contribution to the future of civilization.

As a teacher, you have a challenging responsibility to your students. You direct their learning processes in a way that builds specific abilities and develops a sense of the powers (or weaknesses) of these abilities. You also have the opportunity to help parents understand their roles in the realization of their children's mental potentials.

Whatever role we play in children's lives, our knowledge and our views regarding their education and their mental abilities will either cultivate, fail to address, or perhaps even squelch this great and irreplaceable national resource: the mind of the next generation. It is our responsibility as parents, educators, and taxpayers to empower our children, to develop their intelligences and prepare them for a future we can only imagine.

In the next chapter, I discuss some of the folklore on intelligence and how common assumptions regarding intelligence affect our views of our own and of our children's mental abilities. From there I delve deeper into the scientific views regarding intelligence and examine their influence on the education of mental ability. Once these issues are reviewed, we will (in later chapters) move into basic daily life aspects of raising thinking children and teens.

CHAPTER 4
The Folklore on Intelligence

> I grew up in poverty in a Black neighborhood in the South. For me and my brothers and sisters, intelligence was being smart enough to get out of there any way you could.
>
> thirty-eight-year-old college student

> Intelligence is seen in how a person learns from mistakes, similar to a mouse in a maze. But humans are different then mice. They can learn not only to solve a problem but learn how to problem-solve.
>
> twenty-six-year-old victim of sexual abuse as a child

> I remember being intelligent before I was a [glue] sniffer. I could solve math problems. Now I can't. I killed too many brain cells. I can't think in some ways at all anymore. I feel a part of my brain missing.
>
> eighteen-year-old ex–glue sniffer and learning disabled program student

> Being smart is doing what the teacher wants you to do. All the time.
>
> eight-year-old fourth grader

> I'm smart because my mommy says so.
>
> four-year-old preschool student

So you want to do everything you can to maximize your child's and teen's intelligence. But what is intelligence? Exactly what is it that you want to maximize? We have all kinds of ideas about this thing we call intelligence. And, our ideas regarding intelligence affect us as parents, teachers, policy makers, employees, and young learners as well. So with this chapter, let's take the time to explore people's perceptions of intelligence. Read on, see what you think intelligence is.

UNDERSTANDING WHAT INTELLIGENCE ACTUALLY CAN BE IS IMPORTANT

There are so many forms and definitions of intelligence that parents who want to ensure their children's intelligence must decide for themselves what they think intelligence might be. Parents must also decide which aspects of intelligence they believe are learnable.

Look around. Listen. What do people think that intelligence acts like? How do they recognize it? How do people classify the various types of intelligence? Our definitions of intelligence have a powerful affect on the types of mental ability we encourage in ourselves and in our children.

Let's agree for now that intelligence is some form of mental competence. Let's say that all mental competence can be divided into two basic categories. One of these categories is accumulated knowledge, or expertise: book learning. The other category is control skill or control knowledge: not book learning, but the control of, the use of, book learning (and other information) once it is learned.

The notion of control knowledge is much newer than that of book learning. In fact, our understanding of knowledge and intelligence has undergone marked transition in recent years. Thinking, mental work, can now be explained as a complex but understandable process. This increased emphasis on the process rather than the product of thinking opens up new options for the teaching of intelligence. More and more it is the process of intelligence, the intelligent processing of information, that is emphasized. It is the process of thinking that is considered critical. Throughout this book, I emphasize the process of thinking over the product (or content) of thinking. This in no way means that I deny the value of content. The learning of specific content, of a great deal of specific content, of fact-based forms of expertise, is essential preparation for adulthood. But without intelligent processing and application of that content, it is relatively useless.

MENTAL COMPETENCE NUMBER 1: EXPERTISE

We have a high regard for expertise, or knowledge of content, in the modern world. The measurement of book learning or expertise is a means of designating differences in people's levels of acquired knowledge. We like to rank people this way, and oft for good reason. For example, we want our heart surgeons to be the most knowledgeable on heart surgery. Yet, we too often mistake this measurement of expertise for a sure sign of an individual's mental ability.

Content accumulation, or expertise, is defined as the possession of a body of knowledge, including basic facts (such as how a heart works, 2 + 2 = 4, a cat is a mammal, a hammer is a tool) and various basic procedural information (such as this is how you double a cookie recipe or write a grammatically correct sentence). Expertise is valuable: A student's level of expertise can affect her or his initial state, which can affect her or his capacity to learn more, to assimilate new information. This is because incoming information can be connected to information that has been previously stored. In other words, what one already knows determines, at least in part, what more one can actually learn. So, content accumulation (expertise) is essential. But content accumulation is not necessarily mental ability, except when it is the ability to perform the accumulation itself, while knowing what to accumulate, and the ability to conduct the organization of information that accumulation can involve.

MENTAL COMPETENCE NUMBER 2: CONTROL KNOWLEDGE

Control knowledge, the second category of mental competence, is more complex than expertise. Control knowledge involves many ways of coding and distributing knowledge in the brain. Control knowledge is knowledge directed internally, knowledge working at the deep level of the structure of thinking itself. Control knowledge determines when, why, and how other, more "material" knowledge (or expertise) is used. In other words, the value of what and how much one knows, how much content or material knowledge one has stored, is determined by how adept one is at controlling or performing more complex mental operations with and upon that knowledge.

Young people should be made aware of the distinction between and the importance of both expertise and control knowledge in intelligent thinking. If your child is under the age of seven, you may or may not choose to begin teaching your child the actual scientific terms, expertise and control knowledge. You may simply start with discussions about ways of using one's brain. You may want to differentiate between simple and more complex ways of thinking and build in the scientific terms later. I return to this matter in later chapters, where I examine the process of what we can call *learning to learn*. Here, let me simply say that my purpose here is to encourage adults to talk to children about how their minds work. To do so, educators and parents must be sensitive to their own and others' common assumptions about thinking and knowing.

COMMON VIEWS REGARDING INTELLIGENCE

We can learn a great deal about how children and adults (ourselves included) view intelligence by asking them. I do this by interviewing people. I always find an interesting diversity of answers. Children seem to have, in the main, the sense that intelligence is something that is either learned or practiced (or both) in school. A three-year-old who is perceived as being "very bright" by her preschool teachers explains, as if having said it several times before, that "intelligence is that you are articulate and you know your ABCs." A second child, age seven, claims that intelligence involves "knowing a lot" and "knowing how to get the answers right." Note that both expertise (knowing a lot) and control knowledge (knowing how to get the answers right) are included in her definition. Competence in problem solving is something that young children recognize, appreciate, and talk about (in their own words for the most part).

A five-year-old I am speaking to is a little more explicit when he explains that being intelligent is "when you know what shapes fit, and how to fit them in the right holes, and you can spell words too." In referring to the "how" of fitting shapes into the right holes, he seems to be saying that it's not just what you know, but how you use it. You don't just know that a square block is square, you also know how to determine whether the square block will fit into the round hole. Another perception of intelligence is offered by a nine-year-old girl who says that intelligence is present in those who can "get the answers faster" and are "good at things in class." Again, a child sees competence as more than just having information. She brings in the element of speed—getting the answers "faster."

The ability to "get" answers is more than simply "knowing a lot," having expertise. Although each of the four children includes the notion that intelligence is what you know (i.e., expertise in the form of knowing ABCs, numbers, and so on), three of them definitely see some element of answer-generating or problem-solving competence in intelligence. These are elements of control knowledge. Other more social aspects of intelligence are often found in young people's definitions. The eight-year-old quoted at the beginning of this chapter also views being "smart" as "being able to do what the teacher wants." This idea suggests itself to be a mix of compliance and answer getting. Perhaps knowing where and how to be obedient in school is also intelligent.

Two young ladies, ages fifteen and seventeen (who insisted on talking to me together because they were unwilling to do so alone), go so far as to identify two distinctly different and apparently antagonistic intelligences. The first, what they call "academic intelligence," is not measured on classroom tests but is measured on standardized tests "when they tell you if you've been studying and learning and if you're gifted or not and stuff like that." The second, what they call "social intelligence," is being able "to handle things well" and "knowing how to act in social situations." This type of intelligence "keeps you from getting embarrassed" and "gets you a lot of friends so you'll fit in."

A third adolescent, age fifteen, is quite derogatory about intelligence. For him intelligence is "all mental," has to do "only with school" and is something that "mostly geeks have." Two others, ages sixteen and eighteen (interviewed separately), also see intelligence as being purely academic, but not necessarily undesirable. One says "intelligence just happens to you," while the other says "how smart you are depends on how smart your parents are."

The notion of social intelligence offered by the two girls interviewed together actually implies certain types of problem-solving, or what I will call here *social control activity* in that it involves "seeing what you want (socially) and figuring out how to get it." These adolescents note, however, that when social control intelligence is transferred to a high school physics class, it is not approved of by other students. This form of social control intelligence is described as "kissing up to the teacher" and being a "goodie-goodie" or even a "geek" in some cases. Classroom competencies such as teacher-pleasing and public showing of answer-getting are referred to with negativity by the two adolescents who described social intelligence. In terms of peer acceptance, some intelligent students therefore feel that it is smart to hide their smarts (and sometimes even to "dumb down" to do so).

Young adults tell us about other aspects of the folklore on intelligence. Two women in their mid-twenties explain that intelligence is relative. "If you have street smarts and you don't live in the streets, it doesn't do you any good. Same with caveman abilities. No use these days." One of these young adults, a professional cook, thinks that intelligence includes at least three areas of competence and problem solving: "Survival, communication, and creativity." According to this young woman, some people are born with these abilities, but anyone can learn them with the right teachers and practice. I find it interesting that these young adults sound positive about street smarts while the adolescents sound negative about classroom smarts. Some shift in views regarding intelligence is perhaps evident here.

A twenty-seven-year-old architecture student describes "high intelligence" as a problem solving capability that depends largely on "multidimensional visualization skills." He also includes "the ability to abstract and to symbol-ize" in his definition of intelligence. Here, the notion that intelligence is a problem-solving capacity is explicitly stated. This subject claims that he understands what he is saying about intelligence because he experiences a high level of these abilities in his own mind. He appears to know control knowledge first hand, and to emphasize it even over his obvious vast expertise.

A twenty-eight-year-old professional artist notes that academic intelli-gence is "fine for academics but hasn't helped me much in the real world. I'm fortunate that I also have a natural artistic ability to earn a living with. It's how I express my ideas, work out problems, and support myself. I think that's a kind of intelligence—putting complicated ideas into pictures so everyone can understand them and then earning a living doing it."

Another young adult, who lost his home and all his possessions in a fire, notes that being at peace with oneself is intelligent. He says that he was told repeatedly, "If you had any brains you'd listen" by a teacher. Since then, he has tried to "have brains" and listen very closely. Being peaceful, quiet, and paying very close attention are attributes of real intelligence, he claims. However, he notes that there is more to intelligence. He was told by a sci-entist he met in a Red Cross shelter that he "must have a lot of brains to make it through the trauma of a fire so together." "Coping well is also intelligence," he concludes. "It's survival."

People in their thirties I speak to offer a wide range of ideas about intelli-gence. A thirty-one-year-old computer programmer who is a college dropout and who "went off the top end of the scale on IQ tests all through school" explains that there is a vast difference between what he terms "potential intelligence" measured on IQ and aptitude tests and "actual intelligence," which is manifested in what he calls the "outer" world. He says, "I really only respect and believe in actual intelligence. This is a high level of understand-ing, in the day to day context, of how to apply information to solve problems. If you can't figure out how to use your brains in daily life you don't really have any." In his twenties this respondent had programmed war games for the U.S. Navy and analyzed MX missile trajectories for a scientific corpora-tion. "I'm glad I'm out of the defense business now. But I learned a lot about how to apply math and statistics and science to real life problems in that work. No one really showed me this in school. I was too intelligent to go to college. Education really misses the mark. But now people think I'm slow because I don't have a B.A."

A thirty-five-year-old business woman claims that intelligence is simply curiosity. "The more curious you are, the more intelligent you are. That's all I have to say." She is not interested in continuing the conversation.

A thirty-seven-year-old ranch manager who, in his words, "never bothered to go to college," explains that "intelligent people really listen to what I have to say. They are open to new input. They are able to learn new ways of understanding the world. They are not stuck."

A thirty-eight-year-old college student (quoted at the beginning of this chapter) who grew up "on the really poor side of town" recalls learning that being intelligent was finding a way out of poverty. "Thank God I was smart enough to do that. But now I think intelligence is only intelligence if a person brings information in from many avenues. One kind of information-getting alone is not intelligent. You have to see things from many angles, not linearly. I'm glad I've been going to school as an adult. It's making me learn a new way of seeing things. I can combine this way with my old ways of knowing. This is power. I'm ending up with a lot more than people who didn't come up my way."

A thirty-seven-year-old professor tries to tell me what he thinks intelligence is. After five minutes of beginning sentences and breaking off in the middle of them, he apologizes. "I'm sorry. This is the first time I've realized that I have no idea what intelligence really is. It's an overwhelming question. Does this mean I'm not intelligent?" He laughs nervously.

I encounter considerations of a more philosophical tone among subjects in their forties. One subject, a woman who loves animals, explains that "intelligence is supposed to help a species survive. If we humans are so intelligent, how come we're destroying our ecosystem and threatening our own lives? People forget about animal intelligence. Humans have somehow evolved what they call 'intelligent thought.' Thought has become so important that we don't trust our senses the way animals do anymore." She feels that what humans call intelligence is merely one form of thought, a form with which she is not very impressed.

Another subject, whose mother is a Native American, holds similar views, with an added spiritual element. "Intelligence is trusting your intuitions and having refined intuitions to trust. We get this trained out of us in school. We lose touch with what we really need to know." She also explains that one's intelligence increases as one gains the ability to see things from many different perspectives. "This is the lesson of the medicine wheel. You put something in a big circle you make on the ground. Everyone around the circle sees the same thing differently, from a different angle. In life you have to know where you are in the circle and you have to try to gain as many different perspectives as possible on the same thing. I think that the more you do this, the more intelligent you are."

A forty-six-year-old businessman tells me that intelligence is "thinking clearly and precisely." It is also "mental organization" and "the ability to tackle problems without getting emotional." He goes on to explain that

"many people get emotional or give up on problems, even numerical problems, because they don't have any confidence in their ability to think things
through step by step."

A forty-five-year-old taxi driver claims that "some people are just born stupid. I can find my way around any city. If you give me a few days, I practically
memorize the map. I can see it in my head. That's intelligent."

A forty-two-year-old mother of three tells me that her oldest child is the most
intelligent in school, "But I like to think that each of my kids is intelligent in a
different way. No one can have all the intelligences at once." She also notes that
intelligence in school is the ability to solve the problems the teachers assign,
and that "this kind of thinking may not really be useful later on in life."

As people get older, they may or may not add to their definitions of intelligence. A female administrator in her early fifties tells me that intelligence
is evidenced by how quickly a person can think. A fifty-three-year-old psychologist remarks that intelligence is being able to make "conceptual leaps"
from one level of knowledge to a higher level of knowledge in the same
"domain," or "across domains." Another respondent in her mid-fifties comments that intelligence is "using words and numbers well, remembering
things and using what you know." One gentleman tells me that "there's no
such thing as intelligence. It's only a figment of our imagination. But you
have to be pretty sharp to imagine that it exists and what it's like. Hah."

A fifty-year-old entrepreneur wants to know my "operational definition of
intelligence" before answering my question. When he is told that I have none
to offer him, that I am interviewing people of all ages and walks of life to see
what they say intelligence is, he says then he will create his own definition.
"But first," he says, "if you want to know if someone is intelligent, ask him."
Then he gives me what he calls his operational definition: "(1) having total
recall; (2) crosstalk amongst the categories of information stored in the brain;
(3) making jumps to new conceptualizations based upon that crosstalk; (4)
thinking in four of five dimensions at once; (5) doing all of the above very
quickly." He then tells me that although he can imagine what it is like to have
an intelligent brain, he is not very intelligent.

I interviewed a sixty-three-year-old who was a retired "Documentation
Department Manager" at a large corporation. His tells me his work had
involved "translating highly complex operations, such as those involved in
operating nuclear submarines, into a language that high school graduate
level enlistees in the Navy could understand, and then creating operations
manuals for such purposes." He says that he takes a long time to decide
whether someone is intelligent or not. He lists these elements of intelligence:
(1) An intelligent person is one who "knows a lot about the world—has a

very comprehensive knowledge;" (2) She or he also "has increasingly better ways to put things into perspective;" (3) "The mark of intelligence is that it be always leading toward a higher state of being—being able to cope with yourself and the world in an ever more noble fashion;" and (4) "A lot of hard work is involved in becoming intelligent."

A sixty-eight-year-old man offers yet another view of intelligence. "Intelligence is mindfulness. Mindfulness involves really noticing what the object is, staying intensely aware of and in the present moment. As mindfulness and concentration get stronger, the mind becomes more powerful, more keenly aware, more insightful, more intelligent." According to this man, expertise and control knowledge are part of the thought process. They are appropriate at times; however, they are not really "higher intelligence." They are not steps toward the true "mindfulness" of the highest intelligence. Yet, his conscious application of mindfulness is, in effect, a high level of control knowledge.

WHAT THE FOLKLORE ON INTELLIGENCE TELLS US

Let's summarize these ideas about intelligence. I can see in the comments the people I interviewed made, and in daily life, that a multitude of fascinating notions about intelligence exist. Many, but not all, people's assumptions regarding intelligence are intuitively related to the concepts of expertise and control knowledge.

During the interviews I refer to above, I observed that:

- All but one of my subjects appeared confident about their definitions of intelligence.
- Of my subjects over the age of twenty, most were able to explain at least briefly, their theories regarding intelligence.
- About a third of my subjects elaborated on their definitions of intelligence enough that I could detect distinct components in their definitions.
- Most of my subjects described a component of intelligence that in some way could be interpreted as some form of control knowledge.
- Many of my subjects described a component of intelligence that in some way could be interpreted as expertise.
- I was especially intrigued by the response of the subject who said that, "It takes a lot of hard work to be intelligent." This perception of intelligence as something that the individual can attain through hard work suggests the view that there are or can be degrees of self-consciousness and self-determination in intelligence.

EMPHASIS ON CONTROL KNOWLEDGE MATTERS

My own belief is that to work hard to be intelligent involves knowing what kind of hard work will produce or enhance what kind of intelligence. If one can clarify for oneself what intelligence is, perhaps one can also clarify for oneself how to go about getting it. And this is what parents must do in their own minds when they decide to help develop their children's intelligence. They must clarify for themselves the meaning of (or the various meanings of) intelligence. This must be an ongoing process, because both children and adults can learn more about how their minds work over time. They must also set up clear routes to acquiring the desired intelligences.

The replies of most of the people I quoted in this chapter suggest that they have a sense that something which is, or which can be interpreted as being, control knowledge is a component of intelligence. (Of course they do not use the phrase control knowledge.) Many understand control knowledge to be a mental process exercised upon expertise or "material" (content, "factual") knowledge. Consider some of the ideas about intelligence my interviewees expressed:

Intelligence involves knowing *how* to use material knowledge:

- knowing how to get answers right
- knowing how to fit the shapes
- using words and numbers well

Intelligence involves being adept at controlling or performing mental operations on material knowledge:

- having the ability to solve problems
- using multidimensional visualization
- having the ability to abstract and symbolize
- seeing things from multiple perspectives
- thinking step-by-step
- thinking clearly and precisely
- having the ability to make conceptual leaps
- having cross-talk ability; thinking in many dimensions at once
- having the ability to put things into perspective

Much of this book focuses on the development of control knowledge and on the things that support the development of control knowledge such as positive identity, self-esteem, family support, concentration, brain capacity, and a stimulating collection of early experiences. It is in the development of control knowledge that learning to learn, learning to think, and learning to use information intelligently are ensured (all of which I discuss later in this book). Because control knowledge is more subtle, more complex, and perhaps more fragile than expertise or content knowledge, it is important to emphasize the means of developing such knowledge or intelligence. Above all, it is important that educators, parents, and children become increasingly aware of control knowledge and its applications.

CHAPTER 5

Scientific Definitions of Intelligence and the Freedom of Thought

A lively and impudent gnat was daring enough to attack a lion....

The gnat, hovering over the spot, and sounding a trumpet note of triumph, happened to come in the way of the delicate web of a spider. Slight as it was, it was enough to stop him. His efforts to escape only fixed him more firmly in the toils, and he who had vanquished the lion became the prey of the spider.

Aesop, "The Lion and the Gnat"

Let's dig deeper into this thing we call intelligence. After all, whatever it is, the definitions of it certainly affect us, and our children and teens. This brief chapter discusses some ideas to keep in mind—at least in the back of one's mind—as we go about parenting to raise thinking children and teens. Parents must recognize the tensions affecting their own and their children's teachers' efforts (or lack of efforts) to raise children's mental ability. I have included this chapter to explain some of these tensions, because they are everywhere, although most of us do not say we see them. Some of the concepts I discuss in this chapter are somewhat complex. Some readers may want to return to this chapter once having read the chapters that follow, where specific ways to influence and to raise mental abilities are presented.

NOTIONS OF INTELLIGENCE

The notion that human intelligence can be learned or acquired has become controversial at several points in modern history. Although the once sharp divisions may now have been blurred, education still plays on society's uncertainty and debate regarding the basic source of actual intelligence and mental ability. Although we tend to assume that our schools' educational programs and policies are based on undisputed facts, they are, at the deepest level, driven by belief systems and theories. Thank goodness, the very existence of educational institutions is based on the belief that *something* can be learned in school, that school can teach factual matter as well as thinking processes, both content (expertise), and process (control knowledge). The educator seeks to interact with rather than act upon the student's mind; the mind never arrives in the classroom an entirely blank slate. Were the student's mind to arrive in the classroom an entirely blank slate, education would be a very different task. (Of course, from the moment a child is born, if not also while in utero, experience fills the child's mind with information.)

To think further about this confusing issue in light of our children's education, let's briefly consider this rather impossible science-fiction scenario:

Assume for a moment that, through some feat of genetic engineering, we have rendered the population of students blank slates. Somehow, they all arrive in their first classrooms this way. Students sit, perhaps motionless and robotically obedient, like automatons awaiting curricular programming. Educators recite, demonstrate, or otherwise relay information to students. Students mentally absorb this information, filling their once-blank mental slates. The entire educational process is condensed into a brief chunk of time. Getting educated resembles being inoculated. The student's mind, analogous to the computer, goes in for an injection of programming and a series of data bank installations.

Assume that this futuristic process serves as the guarantor of an eerie form of social equality—as long as every student arrives a blank slate and is fed the same program and the same data, every student knows the same thing, shares the same biases, and has the same abilities. In this particular science fiction world, the opportunities for programming and thus control of thoughts abound. The state mandates that nothing be taught that might enable students to question or to see alternative viewpoints. All officially approved, controlled information and nothing else is distributed to everyone equally. Every student is of the same mind, having learned the same thing. Later in life, when uniformity of knowledge and thought has been ensured in their generation, students are randomly tracked into a higher education aimed at specific training to fill occupational quotas. Still, their uniform mental foundations prevail.

But, then, an unexpected dose of radiation causes a series of genetic mutations, generating some differences in the mental hardware belonging to some of the next generation of students. All students continue to arrive in school with their blank mental slates, but some of their slates are now different, with different areas for different subjects of memory (storage space), and different forms of cross-filing capability. No student's mind is better, just different. The student automatons begin to evidence their individual differences in their learning processes. Educators begin to struggle with these differences. Random tracking of students into specific higher education training is difficult to maintain.

Our imaginary educators decide that all slates are created blank but some are created different from others. They also decide that the goal of education is still to promote as much sameness among everyone, not to recognize differences. But how, they ask? The scientists begin to fight among themselves as to whether or not, and how to, stop the differences. They even argue endlessly about whether or not classrooms (nurture) can override genetic biology (nature) and whether or not nature has any bearing at all on the outcome of education. Without knowing the answer, educators try an array of curricular designs. The students' minds are the handy subjects of massive social experiments, experiments almost too large for them to recognize: school.

Eventually, this science fiction system collapses, because it cannot recognize and cultivate the value of differences and the necessity of these differences.

Today, in our real world, education, along with most social policy, conducts many similarly naive experiments. The modern nature-nurture debate and its various hypotheses emerge, at least in part, from an older philosophical question: Can intelligence exist in the mind apart from environmental stimulation or is it basically acquired and derived from the environment by the senses? And it draws from an even older philosophical question: Can the circle or the triangle (or any concept) exist in the mind without sensory input, or can it only arrive there by way of sensory data drawn from the environment? Is the mind, without input from its environment, merely a blank slate or tablet, an empty vessel waiting to be filled?

This age-old philosophical debate is really quite simple. We have the rationalist (it's all coming from inside the mind) camp and the empirical (it's all coming from the world outside the mind) camp. Extreme rationalists may maintain that reasoning exists in the mind regardless of environmental stimulation. And then the mind imposes its powers of reasoning on all incoming sensory experience. The mind is best suited to know when it relies on its internal reasoning processes rather than on sensory data from the environment. In this extreme, this rationalist view may be a profound model of the inherited or genetically based intelligence perspective. Empiricists, on the other side of the argument, have maintained that to "know" anything is to draw information from the environment: To know is to have a good foundation of externally induced sensory impressions. There is no knowledge without full use of these impressions. This is, in its extreme, the view that may imply that the brain-mind is nothing without its environment. Although various mixes of rationalism and empiricism have emerged over time, they have not diffused the essential differences between these two diametrically opposed views.

SCIENCE AND INTELLIGENCE

And modern science has transformed what was once a philosophical conflict into what sometimes appear to be conflicting facts. On the one hand, some say mental ability may be largely determined by genetic code. Such a troubling position is supported by results of numerous adoption studies, which show that the IQs of children who are adopted at birth are much closer to the IQs of their biological siblings and biological parents than those of their adopted siblings and parents. This suggests that biological (genetically inherited) factors can influence intelligence more powerfully than environmental (adopted family) factors. Studies of fraternal and identical twins support this view. The IQs of twins who are separated at birth correlate increasingly as the twins develop, with the most powerful correlation being between identical twins who, of course, share identical genetic material. The stronger the genetic resemblance, the higher may be the correlation. These findings suggest genetic makeup to be one determinant of intelligence.

On the other hand, intelligence may be so extensively and powerfully influenced by environment that we cannot fully detect the intensity of this omnipresent environmental influence. This influence may extend across the generations through centuries. Perhaps the wrong level of analysis has been applied to the age-old nature-nurture debate. This basic line of argument says that biological determinists, who say that biology determines mental ability, are unwittingly preserving inequality in society. The basic argument also says that biology is not the primary determinant of mental ability. For example, children's low IQ scores can be improved just by telling their teachers that these children are bright but late developers. The effects of IQ and intelligence labeling are implicit but pervasive: labeling preserves a social order in which some children are guaranteed access to the higher echelons of ability and power by being born into the middle and upper classes.

So how do we weed through the jungle of this debate? Well, one answer to this question is that we don't. We skip the debate. Why worry about this thing some call inherited intelligence or inherited mental ability? Let's focus on the *expression of intelligence*, regardless of its origin. The expression of intelligence can be taught and encouraged. It can also be neglected and obliterated. And this is the central issue. It is my view that the more we empower parents, teachers and students to think and to learn, the greater the power of the environment to determine mental ability and intelligence.

MENTAL SUPRASTRUCTURE

The mind processes the information it is receiving by way of the senses in various ways. When working to assess a situation or to solve a problem, the mind actually may build, within itself, a mental model of what it is working on. This mental representation (which much of the time our minds are building without our knowing this building is taking place) is the mind doing a sort of *less-than-obvious-to-the-thinker* form of thinking about thinking. Already, without our realizing it, our minds are conducting forms of higher order or metalevel thinking—control-level thinking. Already then, without our realizing it, our minds are conducting a great deal of *metacognitive activity*. Our fabulous minds are always building mental *suprastructures*. It is there, in the mental suprastructure, that the brain originates and directs mental activity and formats the mental structures that organize and operate on mental activity.

Our realities are defined and labeled and categorized, and then reacted to, by this powerful mental suprastructure. Now that we know this, old nature versus nurture debates regarding intelligence are rather outmoded. Now these debates should collapse into this unified argument: all we know comes both from within and from without ourselves, and our perceptions of within and without are highly interconnected.

So, what I am saying in this book is that if we can get to this mental suprastructure, work with it—if we can consciously and metacognitively nurture it and fuel it—it can become yet more competent, yet more intelligent. After all, anyone's mental ability can arise wherever it does, but once we realize that it already exists, and that the suprastructure for operating it is already present, it is important to handle it well. **Meet your mental suprastructure.**

THE MORAL QUESTIONS

Until we spread the notion that far more can be done to realize children's (and even our own) mental potentials, we will not do far more to realize these potentials. If a parent, or a teacher or a school or a textbook author, assumes that she or he can have a great deal of influence on the expression of a child's mental ability, then an effort will be made to exert this influence. The more we all know about how to enhance the expression of mental ability, the more we will seek to do so and the more effective our efforts will be. The moral question arises: How can we not do everything we can to nurture young people's intelligences? How can we not talk to their mental suprastructures once we know these are at work? It is like having someone come to dinner and be ignored. We do not see the person there at the table. Well, say hello, because that person is the mental suprastructure.

FREEDOM OF THOUGHT

The institution of education prepares the mind to fit into the encompassing social system. The risk inherent in an institutionalized process of mental training is that it may say that everyone should think pretty much the same way. It encourages the homogenization of intellectual activity, or, at least, it favors an acceptable range of and type of intellectual activity within the society. But, in the face of this institutional pressure toward sameness, this homogenization, the preservation of intellectual diversity is critical. A single standard for, definition of, intelligence may be dangerous. We cannot risk eliminating essential and diverse ways of thinking, learning and knowing.

Proponents of both sides of the nature-nurture conflict, and its more modern forms, are missing the point. Although the debate has raged on in all its convolutions, we have overlooked the ultimate question: Is the precious resource, the diversity of intellectual activity, and even of free thought, becoming archaic, an anachronism? Is it slipping away in the fashion that grains of sand leave a hand, imperceptibly until enough is gone for an observer to finally notice the difference? As intellectual diversity and thus free thought leave our grasps, are we increasingly unaware of their loss because we are no longer able to see this loss?

The connection between freedom of thought and the development of children's intelligence is a complex one. It is made at the multiple levels of biological, psychological, social, and political organization. It is at once painfully subtle and grossly concrete, obvious to us. Although freedom of thought is determined by social and political forces, it is empowered by the diversity of intelligence. This diversity allows for diversity of thought. The concept that intelligence exists on a gradient from low to high suggests that the thought processes of some members of the population have higher degrees of mental competence than do those of others. A societal preference for or recognition of a narrow single model of intelligence suggests (even if this is not said aloud) that only the thought processes that manifest that particular intelligence are intelligent thought processes. What a dangerous place to be.

Perhaps the educational system originally existed and may still exist to organize children—citizens—along a narrow continuum of intellect, one that contains the highest potential of a particular intelligence at one end and lesser degrees of that same intelligence down the line. If so, then we as a society are selecting the thought processes best serving that restrictive continuum. People who think, who express their intelligences to a small or a large degree differently, may actually think according to a different intellectual model that exists on a separate continuum. They will, nevertheless, be organized along the official continuum. Freedom to apply alternative intellectual strategies, to put mental suprastructures to work in different ways, and to engage in free thinking itself can become viewed as alien to the social order. Alternative forms of intelligence can go unrecognized, unselected, unexpressed. They can atrophy, suffocate, and die off.

When some of our children and teens seem to be unable to "fit" the system, we must stop to wonder whether our system is unable and or unwilling to fit some children and teens—whether the diversity of mental suprastructures is being repressed and denied. What a dangerous place to be. And how dangerous it is to not know whether or not we are there. How dangerous it is not to know that in each of our heads we house a powerful biocomputer, that each of our own brains is the originator and director of our own personal mental activity, and that each of our own mental structures organize and operate on that activity.

Our social system may not fully see how very unique, special, and essential the mental suprastructures of each of its citizens are. But our young people sense this. And if we really listen to them, really invite them to see their own uniquenesses, the unique workings of their own minds, they will surely show us.

The unlimited capacity of the mind of the human species is here, ready for us to recognize, encourage, and tap into. What we now know about how to think and how to encourage (rather than stifle) real thinking in the minds of our young is only the beginning of where we can go with this. What we do with the minds of today's young people can be the beginning of a whole new avenue in education and in democracy.

A Place Called School (Illustration by Angela Browne-Miller)

Part Two

That Thing We Call School

CHAPTER 6

Modern Education and Intelligence

"There's no use trying," [Alice said]: "one *can't* believe impossible things."

"I daresay you haven't had much practice," said the Queen. "When I was your age, I always did it for half-an-hour a day. Why, sometimes I've believed as many as six impossible things before breakfast...."

Lewis Carroll, *Through the Looking Glass*

On the front lines of education, teachers express many different understandings of intelligence and mental ability. Teachers frequently emphasize the notion that there are many different types of intelligence or mental ability and that no one student has a corner on the market of "smarts." "Every child is special" and "most children will excel at something if given the opportunity" are frequently heard teachers' comments, for which we are ever grateful.

Although most modern teachers express such egalitarian, democratic views regarding their students' abilities, they are likely to be under implicit—unspoken but nevertheless real—pressure to favor certain types of students in their classrooms. It is quite simple: When faced with what can range from fifteen to forty (and more) students, the more cooperative, attentive, responsive students are the most likely to be acknowledged, attended to, and generally viewed as "good" students. Although a "good student" and an "intelligent child" are not always seen as one in the same, the good student is usually regarded as the relatively intelligent or at least cooperative child. And, in terms of academic intelligence as discussed earlier, she or he *is* intelligent *enough*—yes, intelligent enough. Teacher-pleasing is smart, it is rather intelligent, isn't it?

Although most teachers tend to believe that the child's environment has a profound effect on that child's expression of academic intelligence and general mental ability, teachers do not hold the classroom environment entirely, or even primarily, responsible for that expression. I often hear teachers explain that they feel unsupported by families: parents do not help enough or well enough or at all with homework, parents do not emphasize the importance of school, parents do not get involved in school activities, parents do not teach their children to pay attention, parents do not teach their children manners and socially acceptable behaviors, parents send their children to school hungry or sleepy and needing a nap. Yes, parents are guilty as charged—of some of these behaviors some of the time. But parental behavior does not explain entirely children's failure to show mental ability. Some mix of parenting, teaching, playing, television watching, and other factors are responsible. More than this, larger social and economic realities play a huge role. For the most part, every one involved is doing her or his best.

Teachers, quite rightly, want off the hot seat, as do parents. And this is reasonable: Educating children is a team effort. Encouraging children to develop and express their intelligences is also a team effort. One of the products of this team effort is the child's academic performance. Academic performance and mental ability are spoken of almost synonymously these days.

HOW DO TEACHERS SPOT "INTELLIGENT" CHILDREN?

Teachers see some children completing their assignments more rapidly and more correctly than others. These children tend to be (although not always) more attentive in class and to ask the most appropriate questions. "Of course," a teacher explained to me, "there is always the bright child without confidence or the social skills necessary for school success. But those kids are the exception, not the rule."

During my many conversations with school teachers over the years, I have heard various characteristics used to define intelligent children. These characteristics include general curiosity, focused inquisitiveness, continuing interest, and a high degree of alertness:

"The curious students want to know, they want to learn."

"They are interested; they are intelligent."

"I just catch a look of curiosity in the students' eye.... I wait for, I live for, that look. Then I know I've hooked the kid. Then I know I'm really teaching someone, that I've found someone who can really learn."

"Bright kids are awake.... Or, if not, they can be woken up. When I spot 'em, I wake 'em up and then I don't let 'em go."

Some of us believe that all children can be intelligent, it just takes seeing the way to reach them—and the way to help them reach themselves. This is what education is largely about, reaching minds and teaching minds to reach themselves.

BEING "SPOTTED" AS "AVERAGE"

What happens when children are not identified as being intelligent? They are usually identified (even when this identification is unspoken) as being average and then treated as such. Several effects result from being labeled average.

- Teachers' expectations are that the child will perform at a consistently average level.
- The child, receiving few prompts to exceed this level, performs at the acceptable level of average.
- The child comes to view her- or himself as average.
- The parents either express a desire for the child to exceed the demands of being average or accept average academic performance and even reward it.

The last point warrants more discussion here. Whenever parents of a child who has come to be identified as an "average student" demand more than "average academic performance" of that child, the child will likely do some combination of the following:

- meet the parents demands
- feel conflicted in experiencing conflicting sets of demands (excellent versus average)
- feel no conflict in continuing to perform in an average way at school where a critical mass of teachers, fellow students, and even the child all perceive that child as being average
- avoid discovering anything other than average about her- or himself

Another set of possibilities exists here. One, some young people are content and even glad to be labeled as average while hiding their gifts. They may not want to be teased or treated as different, and or they may be unsure of what might happen when adults or other children identify their gifts. Two, some young people choose to enjoy their gifts privately, entertaining themselves without what they expect might be the demands ("harder" classes, more homework, moving to a new class or school and leaving friends, and so on) placed upon them once their gifts are recognized. Three, and perhaps most important, many young people with special abilities have no idea that they have such abilities. They only feel different, even what their peers might call "weird," or they feel nothing at all.

We cannot know, we may not remember, how much pressure young children and even more so teens feel to be the same as everyone else. In the end, being spotted as average can be a relief, and can be a very convincing experience for the child. But "average" is an artifact, an easy label, a statistical statement, a midrange number. Average in human terms is nothing but an artificial reality. No one is this thing we call average.

THE SYSTEM OF EDUCATIONAL TRACKING

Sometimes children are labeled as "below average." As confining as being labeled average may sometimes (but not always) be, being labeled below average is even more restricting. I have seen children of above average and average potential labeled as below average and even as "slow" and coming to buy in to this label for themselves. After a certain number of years of being told that one is mentally slow, and being taught only that which can be learned by someone who is mentally slow, one can begin to assume the characteristics of someone who is so-called less than average. Whether a child is formally placed with other children who are also labeled below average or informally grouped with these children, the label becomes part of the child's self-perception. But what is below average? Below the average of what? If each young person is unique—which each child truly is—then the performance of others is not a measure of that young person's performance. Again, the statistic we call average is merely that—a social or mathematical label, a statistical artifact.

What happens very early in a child's school career can determine the course of that child's life. Once a child is formally or informally (or even only implicitly) tracked onto the slow or average track, the child tends to stay there. Children placed on the fast track may stay there throughout school or only until puberty, when other factors can come into play.

What ever level rears its head, tracking is something that must be practiced with great care and respect—and even some hesitation. Once a child is tracked, his or her reading, math, science, and other lessons are given at one of the tracked levels. A child who spends one year learning math at an average pace may have a difficult time moving up to the fast track in math the next school year. The gap is experienced as too big and ever growing. The children who have been moving at a rapid pace are further along in the content of the math lessons. And, over the years, indeed the gap grows. We cannot always know whether this gap is valid or the product of a series of adult decisions—wise or arbitrary, or simply misguided, or truly neglectful, decisions—which of these, we cannot always know. (And keep in mind that even hidden, out-of-the-awareness forms of tracking take place all the time. Children and teens feel adults develop perceptions, opinions, and expectations about their ability levels, and then these children and teens may actually live out adults' perceptions, opinions, expectations of them.)

GIFTED PROGRAMS

Gifted, exceptionally bright, or exceptionally talented children are also affected by being labeled. We as a society are divided about the meaning and the importance of giftedness. Different school districts handle what they call gifted children in different ways. And within school districts and schools, children are treated inequitably, often causing discomfort to children who have been labeled as gifted as well as to those who have not. Many gifted children experience the discomfort of being treated differently throughout their school years. The label of gifted can be a blessing or a burden. I remember being called "the school brain" in junior high school and being teased and ostracized for being one. I was lonely, lost, confused. The label followed me for years and I eventually decided to suppress my intelligence and reduce my vocabulary when in public to have more friends. Whether the label of gifted is accurately or mistakenly applied, it can hurt. But not receiving the label can be equally detrimental. There are many gifted children out there who no one has noticed; they may receive no special education whatsoever. Parents must know about the various programs available to their children and how children are selected and not selected for participation. Because every child is special, the ideal is to unearth every child's gifts.

Gifted programs take a variety of forms. And people have a variety of feelings about these forms. Programs for gifted children sometimes emphasize education and other times focus on adjustment, isolation, and other psychological issues. There is a lot of disagreement about which is more important. Gifted programs can be regular classroom programs, or special individualized programs, or cluster, group, or pull-out programs. They can be special weekly or daily classes and or entire special schools. Programs that involve more classroom time are not always better programs. Sometimes children who are called gifted become separated from other children in ways that fool them about the world or stigmatize them. At the same time, schools may be forced to select the gifted programs that are least costly or that fit into their budgets most readily, thereby not warranting pulling gifted students away from their social realities. Although giftedness remains a vague and sometimes unfairly awarded label, the true giftedness in everyone is too often missed. Or when seen, responded to inadequately.

Looking at this giftedness issue, each of us must decide what we think—whether giftedness can be fairly tracked and if so how. Services for gifted children usually take the form of either acceleration, enrichment, special grouping, or special guidance:

Acceleration: The advancement of a student in the sequence of elementary and secondary years of school by way of early admission to grade school or college, the skipping or combining of grades and other amendments to the standard program. Acceleration is the least costly form of gifted education as no additional programs are required.

Enrichment: The adaptation or extension of a program to serve the gifted by adding special areas of learning and or learning experiences to the standard curriculum.

Special grouping: The placing together of gifted students to learn at an advanced pace and to motivate and stimulate one another, for all or a portion of the school day or week.

Guidance: The provision of special counseling to gifted students and sometimes to their families, addressing the individual and interpersonal needs typical of gifted youth. This counseling looks at social ostracism, boredom, wanting to be accepted by peers, pressure to be outstanding, conceit, isolation, and family relationships. Counseling and guidance focuses on what we call "affective" development (rather close to the social intelligence discussed earlier). This may be as important or more important than educational efforts, because emotional well-being has a lot to do with the ability to learn and to feel good about learning.

Economic and practical problems affect the characteristics of gifted programs. At the elementary level, special pull-out programs may tend to cost more per student than full-time, self-contained, gifted education classes. Special seminars at the secondary level tend to cost more per student than grouping by subject at the secondary level. This is because, in the latter cases, students more or less exchange one class for another and the school system does not need to develop as special a structure to provide gifted education.

Whether one child is more gifted than another is not the question. If we look, we will see that every child has gifts. Too many of these are unrecognized. Some children just happen to be in the right era of a popular theory, or the right school or school district, at the right time. One of the terrific conflicts for educators and psychologists who conduct and use results of intelligence or even achievement tests to place children in gifted programs is the definition of intelligence as one thing versus the definition of intelligence as multiple things. There are those still today, who even in the face of extensive evidence that there are many intelligences, hold on to the traditional intelligence test with all its biases toward the best test takers as the way to "read" and "label" young people.

HOW THE EDUCATIONAL SYSTEM SEALS A CHILD'S FATE

It is usually some nine years from the time a child enters kindergarten to that child's graduation from eighth grade. During the critical formative years, a child is identified as being of below average, average, or above average academic ability. That child has possibly even been called extroverted, or cooperative and compliant, or withdrawn or trouble-causing. That child has been either purposively or inadvertently labeled. This labeling or framing according to behavioral performance in school molds the child's definition of her- or himself. What ever comes first, the chicken or the egg—the mental ability or the label—no longer is relevant, because labels too often dominate. Alas, we must always remember that young people are not the labels that have been applied to them; they are human beings. Somehow we mix these up sometimes, or our social system does.

This is not surprising. Children spend five-sevenths of the average week at school and, on those days, about half of their waking hours at school. A good portion of the remainder of waking hours on school days are filled with school-related activities: dressing for school, doing homework, participating in formal after school activities, and associating with (playing with, talking with, telephoning) schoolmates. Children's selection of school friends tends to organize around the identification of students with similar social or academic characteristics. Because so many of the characteristics are labeled at school, school defines a large part of children's social lives. In these ways, school exerts a powerful molding influence on a child's identity as much as, and in many cases more than, family—especially as the child grows into her or his sense of her or his mental ability.

The power of social institutions such as the educational system is all-encompassing. The power of schooling is an integral part of the socialization process. School is the institution that prepares children for participation in society (as consumers, as parents, as voters, as labor force participants). Because the machinery of school, and its tendrils reaching into every corner of our lives, is so massive, so far-reaching, parents may find themselves feeling increasingly powerless in determining their children's characters as their children move through the school years. While, at first, in the kindergarten and first-grade years, there seems to be a balance between school and family or even a preservation of the power of family over the power of outside institutions, including school, by second grade many parents report that school life seems to have more influence over their children than family life. Perhaps this is how it should be. I do not express a bias in either direction here. I do contend, however, that parents must make every effort to remain on the front lines of their children's development in the K-8 years, even the K-12 years. They can share that front line position with teachers, faith leaders, coaches, and others in any proportion they choose. But parents must not withdraw. Social systems, including educational systems, are only as sensitive to their individual members as those members keep demanding these systems be.

The key reason for not withdrawing is that our children need defense against institutions. This means that, in a society with a large population and many large bureaucracies, no matter how humanely we feel children (and adults) may be treated, there is the tendency to treat people like numbers. We are all pieces of a large machine we call our social system. A child may therefore receive special attention and care at school, but that child is still one of many children, most of whom are unrelated to each other and to the teachers, and most of whom will spend no more than one school year in close contact with any given teacher. And quite often, our children do not receive special attention and care at school. Instead, they become invisible pieces of a mass. Parents must constantly watch the effect of school on their children. Again, this watching is essential even when a parent is pleased with the child's teacher, classroom, classmates, and school.

How can parents keep an eye on the effects of schooling, of institutionalization, on their children? Parents must make every effort to do the following:

- *Visit the school many times during the year.* If an unannounced visit is considered inappropriate at your child's school, then schedule visits.

- *Be a present parent.* Drive on field trips, attend class events, go to school events. Make your name and face part of the scene. Even if you are an employed parent (which most of us may be), be willing to use sick time, floating holidays, small pieces of vacation time, or exchanged work hours to be at the school at least once a month.

- *Do not miss parent-teacher conferences.* This is the only official time to discuss your child's school performance with the teacher, unless your child is in trouble—and why wait for that?

WATCH FOR EARLY INDICATIONS

Parents must watch for early indications of maladjustment to school in their children:

- *Note excessive complaints about school.* Careful on this one. Most children complain about some aspects of school at some times. What we are looking for here is an ongoing and profoundly negative view of school and everything about it.

- *Note when children feign or fall sick a lot.* When these children actually miss an unusual amount of school, they may or may not be indicating attitude problems. This situation requires a parent's attention. Get the child a full check up, as you do not want to miss any medical problems. If the medical check up reveals nothing, seek a psychological check up. Talk to the teachers about what might be going on at school. And talk to your child, be sure to talk to your child!

- *Note ongoing unexplained tardiness and absences.* Children who, without their parents' knowledge, do not arrive at school on time, do not make it to particular classes, or do not make it to school at all, are asking for someone to notice their fear, their adjustment issues, their learning issues, and or their trouble complying with the rules, trouble fitting in, trouble "being" in the system. Be prepared to respond to this symptom of something with your attention, and proceed as detailed immediately above. Be sure to include a meeting with the teacher or teachers.

- *Note ongoing reports of misbehavior.* Antisocial, aggressive, and inappropriate behaviors at school are, of course, another call for parent-teacher communication.

- *Note consistently low grades.* These are indicative of something. Although attitude problems may be the reason for low grades, it is best for parents to hold back their troubled reactions and most certainly hold back their punishments, Instead seek information regarding the child's perception of her or his own learning abilities. Next, seek teachers' perceptions. Next, if answers are still needed, see a health professional, a doctor, a psychologist, a learning specialist, for example.

SCHOOL-HOME SHOCK

The majority of teachers are quite sensitive to the potentially devastating effects of what I call school-home shock. Specific efforts can be made by both parents and teachers in these areas:

- *Frame, define the difficulty in transition* that children are having. Telling them that this is not unusual, that this happens to some children and that it will get easier is soothing.
- *Establish transitional steps* to help children of any and all ages move through the differences between home and school, and any other differences they are experiencing. These steps should be put in place at home as well as at school.
- *Teachers, have a certain number of minutes* of class time, first thing in the morning, for "phasing in" to the classroom environment.

THE PLIGHT OF EDUCATORS

It is all too easy for us to expect teachers to do more and better work with our children. We do best to remind ourselves that teachers' work is some of the most important, most challenging, and most ambitious work ever done. Teachers teach children; they build an educational foundation of bedrock. Our society depends on teachers to help prepare our children for the future, to ensure the future.

Society has become increasingly dependent on teachers. More and more, both parents are working where there are two parents, and or the only present parents are single and also working. It is important to note also that, twenty years ago, most schoolchildren came from two-parent families. Many of their parents helped them at home, or at least tried to. Those parents, when concerned about what they could do to help their children's educations, had more time to try to provide some of that help. Nowadays, one third to one half of schoolchildren come from families broken by divorce.

This means that, in many geographical areas, 50 percent of all children live with one parent and that about half of today's children have had their family lives moderately or markedly disrupted. They come to school with new problems and new needs. Their single parents may be so busy "keeping it together" that they have to stretch themselves to spend time with their children at all let alone oversee homework. Somehow, parents manage all this and do it well (yes we do). Still, increased responsibility is at least implicitly placed on teachers. And, even in homes where both parents are present, the demands of modern life tend to pull parents away from homework supervision and encouragement regarding school. Even when we think this is not taking place, teachers have to pick up extra responsibilities from all sorts of families, including the families of other teachers (who are also working parents).

Many wonderful teachers are overworked and unacknowledged. Many have had their spirits broken. What a sad state of affairs! We expect a lot from our schoolteachers, including the role of making up for increasingly absent and or stressed and overworked parents. And while we expect so much, we value teachers very little. One of the most obvious indications of this is that teachers are poorly paid. Many other professions are higher on the socioeconomic ladder. The truth is that, if we value our children's teachers so very little, then we value our children, or at least their school days, very little. What are we saying about our own value systems by downgrading schoolteaching as a profession? This is some of the most important work ever done. Why aren't the best and most proven of us recruited into teaching the way we are recruited into other occupations—and then paid as highly as other high demand professions pay?

When we complain about our schools and schools' teachers, it is important to remember that we as a society created and now continue them. Public or private, we pay into their budgets through taxes and tuitions. If we do not like what we see, then it is our responsibility to do more than complain. We must help; and we must get involved.

CHAPTER 7

Choosing and Evaluating Schools

Once you have taken human form, you will never be able to live with your family under the waves again.

The Sea Witch to the Little Mermaid in Hans Christian Andersen,
The Little Mermaid

Schools have a profound effect on the mental development of young people. Good day care and preschool, and good elementary, middle, and high school experiences, help children and teens realize their mental potentials. Not so good and also flat out bad school experiences can have the opposite effect, stifling the young people's mental and moral development, inhibiting their minds from positive growth, sometimes even sending them down the wrong road, suppressing the realization of their mental potential, and shattering their self-esteem.

COST, CONVENIENCE, AND CHOICE

Therefore, choosing a school is a great responsibility. Alas, parents do not always have a choice when it comes to the schools, preschools, and day-care programs their children attend. The three controlling basics, cost, convenience, and choice, are always at work.

Cost: If parents cannot afford to pay the tuition at a particular school or program, their children are not likely to attend it. This is indeed the basic and all too common problem of cost.

Convenience: Even when parents can afford to choose among several educational programs, because the programs are either part of the public school system, or publicly subsidized, or employer sponsored, or church supported, or the parents simply have enough money to choose freely, convenience is a powerful limitation. If the desired program is too far away, if it requires a long commute through congested traffic, if it requires travel in the direction opposite the parents' commute to work, or if the hours just don't fit the parents' schedules, the parents may find it too inconvenient to enroll their children. This is indeed the basic problem of convenience.

Choice: Above all, even when cost and convenience are not issues, choice is a profoundly limiting factor. All too often, parents find that the type of pre, elementary, middle, and or high school experience they want for their children is either entirely unavailable or is so limited that there are long waiting lists and competitive admissions processes. The demand for quality education appears to exceed the supply. This is the basic problem of choice.

These overarching limitations—cost, convenience, and choice in selecting schools—are very powerful. In fact, there really is no full selection opportunity involved for most parents most of the time. They simply have to take what they can get for their children and teens. With this understanding, this book provides special notes for making choices about education wherever possible, and where not possible for knowing what to expect of education for children and teens. Whether looking at preschool, elementary, middle, or high school, it is helpful for parents to know what to look for, what the basics are.

This is why we all (regardless of the age of our children and teens) need to stop and look at the basics of good care at even the most basic—preschool—level, because we all started there (or at least we all started as young children, whether or not we were in preschool). Moreover, parents with older children can see what their children did or did not get in preschool or day care by knowing what a solid early childhood education might look like. We often forget to look back at teens' early childhoods to access whether factors that were present in early years are affecting present time adolescent behavior and learning.

These days, we are more and more aware of to what degree our early years affect our minds as we grow older. This is apparent as we look more and more carefully at early childhood education. Yet, between the factors of cost, convenience, and choice, we may or may not find what we are looking for. In the absence of a large public preschool system, and with so many mothers and fathers of young children in the labor force (or seeking employment), parents need quality day care or preschool more than ever.

Once kindergarten begins, most parents either prefer to or must rely on their local public schools to educate their children. Since most public school districts do not actually offer parents much choice in the way of schools or teachers, as a group, parents of what we call school-age children are exercising less choice than those of preschool-age children. (The law requires school age children to be in school regardless of its quality while preschool is at this point voluntary.) Clearly, cost, convenience, and choice affect us all.

WHAT TO LOOK FOR OR KNOW YOUR CHILD IS MISSING

Look back at what your children and teens have received so far (along the lines of education). If you are the parent of a preschool child, you should be well-informed about the effects of preschool and the characteristics of various preschools before you make your decision about preschool. Getting well-informed can be a problem. There is disagreement among the experts in fields such as early childhood education and child psychology.

Take the debate about "academic" preschool. On the one hand, long-term gains in academic achievement may or may not (depending on who is doing the evaluation) appear great enough to justify parents' financial investments in intensively academic early childhood education. On the other hand, early learning is definitely possible, frequently valuable, and yet many children are not presented with academic stimulation and structure similar to that of school environments in their early years. Early childhood education can help a child enter kindergarten and first grade with both academic as well as social experience (school success in these areas may be linked) and the related independence and confidence. It may also lead to competence in basic reading, spelling, and math.

Where academic and social stimulation at an early age may be valuable, attendance at preschool may or may not, however, be the only valuable means of acquiring this stimulation. Children also can acquire these experiences at home, engaging with their parents, watching older siblings do school work, and in many other ways.

SOMETIMES BEING HOME IS BETTER

And sometimes academic or any preschool is not right for a child. There are times when this may not be the preferred approach. In fact, the effects of academic pressure on preschool children can be, when too intense, psychologically damaging. Yet, highly structured and regimented early childhood education can translate into perceived or actual pressure on young children—pressure that may embed itself in the mind of the child and then linger throughout the childhood and adolescence years (or longer). Where great emphasis on achievement and measurable progress is experienced at a very young age, "work hard, do well and this is good" may be learned, and the threat "do not work hard, do not do well, and this is bad" may also be learned. Because young children have not yet mastered much self-discipline, the external discipline that may be applied and expected in intensive early childhood educational programs may be too extreme. We must always remember that young children can be damaged by stress just as can adults. Early childhood education may benefit young children simply by teaching them to learn and to respond to structure rather than by teaching them to excel at specific skills, in essence, to excel or else.

NO SINGLE ANSWER

Clearly, there can be no single correct answer regarding preschool or not for all children. As a parent, you must make your decision about early childhood education personal. Ask yourself:

- Am I setting standards for my child that are unrealistically high or low?
- Whose standards are these? Mine or those of others?
- What are these standards for?
- Do these standards make sense to me?
- Do I want my child to be an early achiever, a "superbaby?" Do I want this because that is what my friends want for their children? Or because that is what I want for my child?
- If I want my child to be an early achiever, do I want this because this is what I was or wish I had been?
- If I want to encourage my baby to be a superbaby, is there only one way and only one type of super that my baby can be?
- What choice will help my child be happiest and healthiest in the present? Is this important to me? How important?

Your decision regarding preschool should never be final. Monitor your child's well-being at and interest in preschool on a regular basis. Know that many children with some preschool experience adapt to kindergarten and first grade more readily than do children who leave home for the first time at age five. It is also true, however, that children who enter full-time, out-of-home day care by age one and remain in such care until kindergarten may have discipline, concentration, and other learning problems in elementary school. In the end, we must see that reactions to out-of-home care and school experiences vary child by child. Pay close attention to the effects of all activities on your child. Where you have little or no choice, be sensitive to your child's reactions and to everything your child tells you in words and in actions, because these are expressed in a variety of ways and emerge in the present and over time.

Many parents consciously choose to de-emphasize the educational aspects of preschool and turn to day-care programs instead. Day-care and preschool choices are matters of personal preference. Being clear on what your preferences are will help you choose a program. You may not find a program that satisfies all of your preferences, but you will at least have some criteria for making a choice. Keep in mind that a day-care program may look like all play, snacks, and naps, and may indeed be this combination of activities in a social (group) setting, which is actually quite valuable in development.

For parents who are past the early childhood stage, look back on your child's early childhood. Look for what your older child or teen may still be dealing with as a result of what she or he did and did not experience in early childhood!

A PARENT'S PREFERENCES MATTER

Look back on the following, or do the following: List all your personal preferences in the day-care or preschool arena and organize them in order of their importance to you. Some preference areas I recommend that you include are:

Love and affection. Are you looking for a place that emphasizes one-to-one love and affection between staff members and your child to encourage the child's sense of security away from home? Or do you prefer a program with a more social emphasis, where children learn to feel at home in a group and also independent around peers? Maybe you prefer a mix of these approaches.

Educational approach. Do you want formal education or informal education for your young child? If you prefer formal education, do you want a mix of subjects or a special focus such as music, acting, or art, or perhaps a spiritual or religious focus reflecting the family preferences? Whatever this might be, consider what subjects are important to you, such as reading, mathematics, music, foreign languages, and art. If you prefer a less formal learning program, what kinds of activities would you like to see your child involved in? And, at what age do you want your child to begin these activities?

Religious orientation. Religion or no religion? Is a religious or a non-religious approach a high priority for you? If you seek religion for your child, do you prefer a particular religion or an interfaith approach? Do you want a program operated by a religious organization of your choice? Do you have a choice in your area?

Child preference. Do you have a sense about which program your child might prefer? This is a difficult question, and this is something that you must continue to ask yourself and your child as your child grows. Do not expect your child to know right away whether a particular setting or program is right for her or him.

These are just some areas of preference. Other areas of personal preference that are important include discipline, food, nap time and its length, the age range of children at the school, the ethnic composition of the group, the ages of the staff, the qualifications of staff, the location of the day-care program and its cost, and more.

Selecting a preschool or day-care program also requires careful attention to safety and protection matters. Some of these are:

Safety of the grounds. Can the children get into the street? Are there places where they can fall? Is the building ventilated? Are there an adequate number of exits?

Safety of the equipment and the toys. Is the playground equipment in good repair? Is it sharp and rusty? Are the toys safe for children your child's age?

Staff-child ratio. Are there enough adults to pay attention to each child's safety?

Cleanliness and hygiene. Are the bathrooms clean? Are the tables and chairs clean? Is the place regularly cleaned? Do the staff members wash their hands often and thoroughly and ask the children to do the same? What are the rules about sick children? Are sick children separated from the well children? Are they sent home? What would you like to have happen?

Licensing. Does the program operate under a license? If it does not, why not?

The decisions parents make about their preschool-age children are some of the most important decisions they will ever make. The preschool experience can mold a child's later adjustment to elementary school. Always pay attention to your heart and your mind when you visit a preschool or day-care program. The well-being of today's preschoolers affects the well-being of tomorrow's world.

This discussion is important even if your child or teen is older. Think back and ask how each of the above pre-school and or day care factors, as well as the questions presented at the end of this chapter, may have influenced your child's and your experience of early childhood care, whether it was day care or preschool or some combination of both or something other than this. Is your child or teen still affected by these factors? You can even evaluate your child or teen's present day school along these lines, with some adjustments.

LISTING PREFERENCES

I have included at the end of this chapter a checklist for parents who seek guidance in making such important choices, which I call Choices: A Model [Childcare and Preschool] Checklist. You can modify this list to fit the school age and needs of your child. You can also modify this list to fit your personal opinions about what makes day care, preschool, and school good by adding, taking out, or changing questions. Ask the questions that best express what you are looking for in a program.

Use your list of questions like a score sheet. Before using this checklist, make several copies of it and then fill out one copy out for each preschool or day-care program that you are considering. Total each score sheet so that you have your own rating for each day-care or preschool program. If you have asked yourself the appropriate questions, the program with the highest score will be the best for you.

Answer each question by circling a number from one through five. A five is the highest score you can give. It means that you feel very good about a school or program in the category that the question asks about. A three is an in-between, neutral score. A one is the lowest score you can give. It means that you do not feel good about a school or program in the category the question asks about. Questions are not listed in order of importance.

Again, there are many items other than those listed on the checklist to consider. Remember to check the program for a current license and its liability insurance. Check the history of the program: how long has it been there, how much turnover has there been among children and staff? If the program rents or leases space, what is the duration of the rental agreement or lease? Could it shut down on you when you need it most and after your children have become attached to it?

Take time to review the programs you might or will (or have already) placed your children in. There is much about preschool and child care that is difficult to assign a score to, or to score at all, let alone quickly. It is good to visit the program more than once. I learned this early on. I once visited a program that received rave reviews from parents and top professionals. I, myself, was impressed at the outset. But, the next day, when I drove by, I saw one of the child care workers from the program walking down the street with nine children from the program. She had no other adults with her. The children were not holding hands and they were stepping in and out of the street. The traffic was very heavy and the children were clearly out of her control. Yes, a high scoring program was failing in the very basic area of safety. (I had to stop and get out and help. How could I not?)

Many parents of preschool-age children are now weighing the financial and career essentials (or rewards) gained when both parents work away from home against the loss of irreplaceable contact with and closer supervision of their children. There is no single right way or single wrong way or easy solution for any of us. This is one of life's decisions, a choice that parents must make. And, as I noted earlier, all too often, there is no choice. Economic necessity and long child-care and preschool program waiting lists leave parents with few real options. They feel forced to place their children in any affordable and available program.

SELECTING AND EVALUATING SCHOOLS
FOR CHILDREN AND TEENS

If you are in a position to be actually choosing an elementary, junior, or high school for your child, you are fortunate. Many parents have no choice regarding the K-12 education of their children. In choosing a school, or in reviewing the school you already do use, consider some of these aspects.

The atmosphere. Gauge your and your child's reaction to:

- the philosophy of the school
- the sense of community
- the sense of safety and security
- the school's responsiveness to diversity
- the school's responsiveness to cultural backgrounds
- the school's responsiveness to individual needs and temperaments
- the involvement of parents, family members

- the degree of cooperation among teachers, the staff, and others
- the relative mix of cultural characteristics among both the students and the teachers
- the mechanisms available for answering parents' questions and concerns and for hearing children's or their parents' complaints

The structure. What is your and your child's reaction to:

- the attention to discipline, limits, and rules
- the clarity of rules and behavioral boundaries
- the amount of structured learning time built into the daily program
- the use of psychological screening and academic tests

The psychology. What is your and your child's reaction to:

- sufficient personal involvement on the part of teachers in their teaching activities, including an adequate amount of one-to-one, personal attention delivered with appropriate affection, warmth, and physical contact
- the extent to which teachers effectively manage psychological upsets and traumas
- the degree to which transition times (arrivals and departures of children) are smoothly planned and executed

The education. What is your and your child's reaction to:

- the clarity of educational philosophy and program design
- the effects of any preenrollment screening for mental or education level (the procuring of attention to treatment for those identified as children with special learning issues, and the use of special classes for the gifted or those with special needs or interests)
- the degree of sensory and mental stimulation
- the adequacy of academic instruction
- the opportunities for creative expression
- the training in practical skills

There are no right or wrong responses to this list of some of the many characteristics of school. Everyone has her or his own preferences when it comes to schooling. So much goes into the selection of a school. Although curriculum is very important, a good curriculum in a terrible atmosphere is not going to provide a positive school experience. On the other hand, a wonderful and loving school environment in the absence of any activities purposefully encouraging mental development may not be what most consider "true" school.

When I evaluate a school, I want to know something about each of the items I listed previously, and more. I also take a very close look at the success of the school in terms of averages and ranges of the children's achievement test scores. Achievement test scores may say something about how well academic material is being taught. And whether or not we want them to, our children's test scores can matter. Although standardized test scores do not tell the whole story, they do determine the school placement and school admissions futures of our children and teens. If the school I am evaluating has a low achievement test average compared to the average on the same test at other schools, I know that the children graduating from the low average school may not be getting the help and education they need and are therefore having difficulty testing and competing, at least on paper. Again, test scores are not everything. In fact, I do not favor standardized tests as the primary means of assessment. But test scores are powerful. They talk. They follow our children. And they are, whether or not we like them, convenient.

One thing I try to avoid in my evaluation of a school is looking at its overall student body grade averages. Parents tell me they ask schools about their overall averages quite often. Grade averages mean very little in terms of the quality of the school. A school can have an overall student body grade average of A-, but this does not necessarily mean that the school is doing a fantastic—or even adequate—job of educating all of its students. It may mean that the school grades much too easily. It may mean that the school inflates the grade averages so that the school will look good and so that more of its students will be admitted to elite high schools and universities. I have seen this, especially at the high school level, all too often. I have found many public and private high schools guilty in this area. And the children, the students, are the ones that are hurt by this. A child who is earning C's and is, instead, being given B's or B+'s or even A–'s is therefore being misinformed about the world out there. I see college freshmen in tears, claiming, "I was an A student in chemistry in high school and now I am a C– student, and I am studying much harder now. Why is this happening to me?" In many cases, this is happening because the high school let its students believe that they were performing at higher levels, studying more and learning more than they actually were. Although this may be a pleasant illusion for the student while it is happening, this student may pay in serious ways later—unless something is done to help this student along the way. Simply grading higher does not prepare the student for the future. There are many ways to build confidence, and surely awarding a good grade for achieving a personal best is a good idea; however, it must be made clear that this is what this grade is reporting.

Visit the classrooms of the schools you are evaluating. Watch what happens there. Do you like the vigor, the structure, the content, and the spirit of the teaching in each subject? Does your child? Talk to the parents and students who are currently involved with the school. How do they answer the questions I ask in this chapter? Most important, talk to as many graduates and parents of graduates of the school as you can. They will tell you a lot that the school will not say—both positive and negative. Remember, you and your child are the consumers of education, and you have a right to be a well-informed consumer.

Model (Childcare and Preschool) Checklist

(This checklist can be adapted to serve as a checklist on K-12 schools.)

Suggestion: Build your own checklist using these and your own questions. This list can be adapted to elementary, middle, and even high school with some attention to specific questions that you may want to replace.

Directions: Go over the questions in this checklist, adding or changing questions where you want to. Then, make a copy of this checklist, several copies if you are evaluating more than one preschool or school for your child or teen. Rate each preschool or school according to the questions below. The lowest score, a "1" in response to a question, will be your lowest or least best feeling about this preschool or school in the area of the particular question. The highest score, a "5" in response to a question, will be your highest or best feeling about this school in the area of the particular question. If you feel neutral, or that the school is average in the area of a particular question, choose a score close to the "3." You will add all the scores together at the end of this questionnaire, to see how you score this preschool or school. You can rate several preschools or schools this way, and then compare the total score you have given each one, to see how they compare.

How good do you feel about:	Do Not Feel Good About		Feel Neutral About		Feel Good About
1. The cleanliness of the place where this program operates?	1	2	3	4	5
2. The safety of the environment?	1	2	3	4	5
3. The safety of the neighborhood?	1	2	3	4	5
4. The quality of the toys?	1	2	3	4	5
5. The amount of space available per child?	1	2	3	4	5
6. The meals and snacks fed to the children?	1	2	3	4	5
7. The general health of the children enrolled in this program?	1	2	3	4	5
8. The general health of the staff who work in this program?	1	2	3	4	5
9. The time spent on physical activities?	1	2	3	4	5

	1	2	3	4	5
10. The balance of males to females among staff?	1	2	3	4	5
11. The balance of males to females among children?	1	2	3	4	5
12. The age range of the staff?	1	2	3	4	5
13. The age range of the children?	1	2	3	4	5
14. The way the rules are enforced?	1	2	3	4	5
15. The opportunities for family involvement?	1	2	3	4	5
16. The overall educational philosophy?	1	2	3	4	5
17. The types of educational activities?	1	2	3	4	5
18. The amount of time spent on prereading skills?	1	2	3	4	5
19. How well prepared the staff are to teach children?	1	2	3	4	5
20. The amount of quiet time?	1	2	3	4	5
21. The amount of nap time?	1	2	3	4	5
22. The amount of one-to-one attention children get from staff?	1	2	3	4	5
23. The amount of affection children get from staff?	1	2	3	4	5
24. The distance of this day care program from your home?	1	2	3	4	5
25. The distance of this day care program from your workplace?	1	2	3	4	5
26. The hours this program is open?	1	2	3	4	5
27. The salaries of the staff?	1	2	3	4	5
28. The cost of this care?	1	2	3	4	5
29. The overall quality of this day-care program?	1	2	3	4	5

A Place Called Preschool (Courtesy of Angela Browne-Miller)

CHAPTER 8

A Note on the Issue of Neglect and Abuse in Day-Care, Preschool, and School Settings, Including Inattention to Bullying

> Looking back, I know I was afraid to tell anyone what was happening to me. But I am not sure I was aware I was afraid during the time it was taking place. I think I was just going blank to deal with it.
>
> young adult who experienced sexual abuse as a child

Here we will talk briefly about the possibility of neglect and abuse in day care, preschool and K-12 school settings, including something not often considered abuse—inattention to bullying. Before beginning, some important notes: First, for purposes of this discussion, we do include neglect in the range of abuses, as neglect is indeed a form of abuse. Second, where child to child bullying or other abuses of children by children (I am including teens here) is taking place, this must be identified and addressed by teachers and school officials. Where this is not addressed, this is neglect, and in essence, the teacher's or school official's indirect abuse of the children being bullied (as well as of the children bullying who need help to stop bullying). Third and very important as well, the **majority of instances of adult to child abuse occur in the home** rather than in child-care, preschool, and or school. Nevertheless, there are instances of adult to child abuse in settings away from home, with grave and frequently traumatic consequences for the child or teen being abused. We begin with this third area, adult to child abuse, below, and return to bullying later in this chapter.

THE CHOICE TO MONITOR

Even when parents have no choice as to which program or school their children attend, parents do have a choice as to whether or not they monitor its quality including its safety. If you do not feel comfortable discussing this matter with your child's teachers and or school officials, this requires even more of your attention, as schools should invite your interest in these areas. I have suggested many elements of quality in the previous chapter. The opposite of the quality of care of our children is also important. Many parents are indeed concerned about the possibility of child neglect and abuse in out-of-home care, preschool and even K-12 school settings, because neglect and abuse can have serious negative effects on a child's physical and mental development, in fact can be quite traumatic with long lasting effects.

This may be of special concern for parents of children who may be too young to report to their parents, or to even know, when they are being neglected and or abused. Yet even children and teens old enough to report abuse may not for fear of being blamed for it, embarrassment, social stigma, and worse. In some cases children (of any age) who are being abused are threatened in such a way that they fear telling anyone about the abuse.

First, let me say again that the rates of child abuse in day care, preschool, and school are very low when compared to the rate of child abuse occurring in children's own homes. Some people may claim that this is because child abuse in day care and school is more under-reported than child abuse in the home. However, abuse is more likely to take place behind closed doors. Day-care and preschool settings are generally more public than private homes. Parents pick up their children at various hours of the day and sometimes drop in unannounced. Children themselves are often aware of what is happening to the children around them.

If your child-care, preschool, or school program does not allow unscheduled or even scheduled visits from parents, you would do well to inquire immediately as to why. You have a right to know what goes on there. You have a right to visit. Still, parents dropping in unannounced at any hour of the day can be disruptive. So please, please do not view scheduling requirements as signs of problems, let alone signs of abuse. But make certain that you

Anybody Home? (Courtesy of Angela Browne-Miller)

visit, and more than once. And do drop in a few times during the course of the year.

Another note. Children go through many different phases of personality development. Some blatant changes in a child's temperament, including fear and mood swings, are to be expected as a child grows and experiences new aspects of the world. Sudden expressions of dissatisfaction with day care or school may simply be normal developmental expressions. On the other hand, parents do well to remain alert to such changes because they may be indications of problems.

SIGNS

Here are some signs that may indicate abuse, which usually when there is abuse do not appear alone but in clusters of these and other symptoms:

- When a child cries and resists going to preschool or day care, or when an older child just will not go to school, be careful not to jump to conclusions. This sort of behavior is a common behavior, one many children exhibit for a variety of reasons. However, some children are indicating that there is a fear of going to day care, preschool, or school. Watch this closely, examine this sign. Screen for other indicators as well.

- Refusing to go to school plus unusual shifts in a child's emotional interactions with parents, such as surprising shifts in responses to parental affection, or the child's withdrawal, and or unexplained anger, are also something for parents to be aware of. Again, be careful not to jump to conclusions.

- When a child appears unusually frightened of a caregiver or teacher, this is also something to examine. And again, be careful not to jump to conclusions.

- When a child has unexplained marks, abrasions, wounds, and or other injuries, this is of course something to examine. Especially when these injuries are atypical of child's play, these are something to be aware of. Repeated injuries are an added alert.

- Wounds, bruises, and or bleeding in the genital areas, difficulty sitting, and urinary tract infections can be signs of abuse as well. Again, do not jump to conclusions.

- Any repetition and or clustering of these and other symptoms should catch a parent's attention.

WHEN A PARENT IS UNCOMFORTABLE
FOR ANY REASON

When a parent is uncomfortable for any reason, the parent should follow up on this perception. Although many parental anxieties are merely parental anxieties, there is nothing wrong with being concerned about and aware of one's child's well-being. If you feel there may be a serious problem, visit the teacher (or caregiver if this is day care rather than school or preschool). Rather than go alone to discuss your concerns about certain symptoms, take someone with you, perhaps the child's other parent or a close friend or family member. If you feel that the caregiver or teacher responds to you in an overly defensive, angry, standoffish, or unusual manner, continue the conversation if you can, seeking some sort of connection and idea of what the caregiver or teacher believes might be the source of these symptoms you are discussing. If you are suspicious after this conversation, truly feel that there is some form of child abuse taking place, contact the local Child Protective Services office; if this is not possible, then contact law enforcement.

SUSPECT ABUSE WITH CARE

Be careful when you suspect abuse. Abuse is only one of the possible attitudes or problems a child or teen may be expressing when she or he is upset about going to school, preschool, or day care. Maybe other stressful changes have occurred. A new person on the staff? New children in the class? A favorite friend gone? A new room? Increased competition for toys, books, or attention? Aggression between children? Bullying?

And what about the child's life at home? Has anything happened in your home life in recent months? Family breakup? Domestic violence? Money worries? Unemployment? Moving to a new neighborhood? New fights with a sibling? Birth of a new child? Drug or alcohol problems? Other potential stresses? These things are felt by children as well as adults. It is quite possible that a child may express feelings about family problems by projecting them onto the daycare, preschool, or school situation. And, without realizing it, many parents would choose to think that the day care or school environment is the source of the child's anxiety rather than believe that family life has caused the child to be upset.

Where the children are of preschool age, many working parents feel some degree of guilt about leaving their young children in the care of non-family members for all or a portion of the day several days a week. Quite often, we parents are not fully in touch with the guilt that we feel. But, somewhere deep inside, there is a sense that we are neglecting and perhaps even abandoning our children by dropping them off and leaving them in the care of someone else who we don't know extremely well. In most cases, parental guilt about preschool and day care is most apparent when parents first enroll their children in the program. Soon both parents and children grow accustomed to the arrangement. Many children even grow to love the teachers and school or program staff, and also the peer contact, they receive there. This may sometimes leave parents with almost invisible, subtle, unac-knowledged, deeply buried feelings of hesitation or even resentment about leaving their children. By elementary school, most parents are over these feelings, but they may still feel uncomfortable about their choice—or lack of choice—of school for their children. Or about the amount of time they have to be involved with their children's schools.

Most of the childcare, preschool, and school staff I have met are wonder-ful, giving people. Get to know the people who work with and teach your child. How do you feel about them? How does your child relate to them? Take the time to get your questions answered. Examine closely your reac-tions to your child's teachers or caregivers, and any of your own guilt regard-ing your placing your child in their care (at what may seem a young age to you and maybe too young in your eyes). And again, if you are left with con-cerns about child abuse, then the situation warrants more of your attention. Pay attention to this, if for no other reason then that you need to put your-self at ease.

FURTHER SYMPTOMS

Having said all this, we must also admit that some child abuse and neglect do occur in the day-care, preschool, and school settings and that this can be extremely damaging to its victims as well as to the other children who see or sense it happening. Just seeing my school principal beat a boy who was misbehaving in my third-grade class ruined the rest of the school year for me. And I was not the one who was hit. I was one of the ones cowering at my desk. Child abuse is one of the most despicable crimes imaginable. It is important for all of us, whether parents or not, to be on the lookout for the signs of child abuse.

Let's take a closer look at symptoms of abuse. Physical abuse is relatively easy to spot. If a child has bruises, welts, lacerations, burns, or broken bones that seem to go far beyond what she or he would receive in normal child's play, be alert to the fact that she or he may be enduring some kind of extreme physical aggression. These may be unusually severe, or unusually repetitive, or unusually placed and shaped bruises or wounds. Of course, look with care, because it is extremely easy to mistake abuses for injuries and vice versa. Also note that if this is abuse, it could be adult to child abuse or it could be child to child abuse.

Extremely disturbing experiences such as physical violence usually result in behavioral indications such as reversion to bedwetting in a young child who has quit wetting the bed (usually seen in children under seven years of age), wincing or jerking away when other children or adults approach or reach to touch them, extreme fear of a person or place, extremes in behavior, or unexplainable mood swings, including listlessness, detachment, and aggression.

Sexual abuse is a difficult topic and more likely to take place in nonschool, mostly familial or close to familial settings. Such abuse can be the result of adult to child abuse, or of child to child—perhaps older or more promiscuous child to younger child—abuse. Indications of sexual abuse may include those just described and also more specific signs. If a child has been sexually abused, you may see that the child has difficulty in walking or sitting, experiences pain when urinating, and has pain, swelling, itching, bleeding, or discharge in the genital area. Signs of venereal disease can, of course, also be indications that sexual abuse has occurred. Also be alert to sudden changes in sleeping or eating habits, poor peer relations, poor self image, or abrupt changes in school performance.

Children who have been or are being sexually abused may exhibit some of the changes in behavior that children who have experienced physical violence exhibit. You may also find excessive nightmares about which the child cannot be consoled, compulsive masturbation, and bizarre, sophisticated, or sexual behavior beyond the child's years. Remember, all of these symptoms may be symptoms of abuse. But they can also be symptoms of other stressful events in a child's life. Note: the child showing sexual behavior at an early age may not be the result of a form of actual physical-sexual child abuse. Exposure to Internet, video, and print pornography can also be abusive. In fact, showing children pornography is a form of child abuse, and is defined as such by law.

Children usually let us know that they are going through something when they are. We adults do not always know how to correctly read or recognize the signs. We have to learn to hear or see what children are telling us. Sometimes, other children will report that a child is being or has been abused. And, sometimes, a child will reveal that she or he is being abused by telling part of the story or by saying that there is something she or he cannot tell.

Listen to your child. And listen to yourself. You may already know what you need to know.

Whether the problem that your child is experiencing is the result of abuse or of something else, if you continue to feel concerned about abuse and neglect, seek a professional assessment of your child's condition. Any time you are worried about your child's adjustment to school or preschool, follow up on this concern by talking to the child, other children, the teacher, other teachers, other parents. Again, take your child to professionals such as psychologists or medical doctors if your concern continues.

A NOTE ABOUT SEXUAL ABUSE BY CHILDREN AND TEENS

No discussion of the neglect and abuse of children can avoid the discussion of child to child abuse. While we are quite rightly concerned about child abuse by adults, we must also address what children and teens do to children and teens, both at school and at home. Many of the signs and symptoms of, and suggested responses to, adult to child abuse listed above are relevant in instances of child to child abuse. Parents and teachers do well to review the above again, in light of the child to child abuse perspective.

Sexual abuse of children and teens by children and teens is complex. We must be alert to its existence, and again, review all the above information regarding signs and symptoms. We must also note that there are many forms of this abuse, ranging from simple sexual pressure teens (and younger children) put on each other, to the circulation of nude pictures of each other, to other more overt forms of abuse such as rape, date rape, drugged rape, and ritual rape. Parents and teachers do well to learn about these forms of abuse and to be on the watch for them. Far more of this is taking place than adults realize. It is best to arm young people with information on how to defend themselves, what to be aware of, what to stay away from, what to report to an adult. The matter of young people abusing other young people—and of young people abusing themselves—requires an in depth discussion, and a great deal of parent and youth education. Here, the purpose is to alert parents and teachers to the gravity of this problem.

BULLYING OR PEER ABUSE AND ITS NEGLECT

Another form of child and teen to child and teen abuse is bullying or what is also called peer abuse. Bullying is a very serious problem; adults must be aware of and alert to it. If not addressed, the effects of bullying can be quite harmful and sometimes even lethal. Bullying is the act of intentionally causing harm by means of coercion, manipulation, harassment, threats, and or actual physical assault. More specifically, bullying can include but is not limited to: physical aggression such as shoving, poking, pinching, scratching, biting, hair pulling, slapping, punching, kicking, beating, stabbing; social aggression such as name calling, teasing, gossip, mocking, ostracism, ignoring, social isolation, and criticizing dress, gender, race, religion, disability and so on. The bully typically is seen (by the bully and often also by the bullied) as having some form of dominance or entitlement to dominate, whether it be physical size and or strength, willingness to be violent, social power or other sense of superiority over the victim (or target). The bully also typically has been bullied or abused at home or by an adult or other child or teen bully. Of note is that characteristics and acceptability of bullying do vary across cultures.

Many of the signs and symptoms listed earlier in this chapter may be indications that bullying is taking place. Bullied children frequently exhibit fear, loneliness, isolation, depression, sleeplessness, ongoing physical pains such as stomach aches, and unexplained injuries. (Of course, these symptoms do not say for sure that bullying is taking place.) Being bullied can have a powerful and negative impact on a child or teen's schoolwork, learning processes, social development, mental health and physical health. Quite often, the very process of being bullied means that the bullied child or teen does not let adults know that the bullying is taking place, for fear of more and greater bullying.

Parents and teachers must educate the children they live with and work with about bullying, about its definition, its signs, and most importantly, that it is absolutely wrong. Young people who are being bullied must know how to ask for safety, and that reporting the bullying will not result in further and worse bullying, but rather protection and a solution. Adults who look away from bullying are neglecting the children and teens they are responsible for. This neglect is, in itself, a form of abuse. Although bullying is becoming illegal in many areas, the legal aspects of an adult neglecting child to child abuse via bullying is still being formed.

Many schools have begun anti-bullying programs, with significant success. If your schools do not have such programs, urge the establishment of these. Also, make sure bullying is discussed at home. Encourage open dialog about what is going on among the children and teens who come into contact with your child and or teen. The neglect of bullying is not only harmful to the person being bullied, it is also quite harmful to the bully. If patterns of abusing and of being abused are not halted in the childhood and teen years, these can linger and become still more dangerous in adulthood.

CHAPTER 9

Easing the Transition from Home to School

Once I was a marionette, as I am now, but I did not like to study and I ran away from home. One day I was changed into a donkey....

Pinocchio to the poor man who bought the donkey in Carlo Collodi,
Pinocchio: The Story of a Marionette

The explicit purpose of school is to educate, especially to educate in cognitive, physical, and social areas. No matter how relaxed and undirected a classroom may be, it is most definitely a formal learning environment in that it is not taking place in the home. The formal learning environment has, quite naturally, the effect of formalizing learning. This may seem an obvious deduction, but do we know what it is that actually happens when learning is moved from home to school, when learning is formalized?

Again, we (all of us, children, teens, and adults) are always learning. Just getting through a day, an hour, a minute, involves taking in information about new things and also about not so new things. Even the reinforcing of existing patterns involves some form of learning. So informal nonschool learning is taking place all the time.

THE CHILD IN THE FORMAL LEARNING ENVIRONMENT

When a child begins to attend school, learning becomes connected with that setting: school. Although learning occurs in all settings, and not just in school, much of the non-school learning occurs so informally that it can take place unbeknownst to the learner (and also unbeknownst to the person, pet, or object "doing" the teaching). By contract, in the school setting, students are told, "Today (or this week, this month, this semester) we will learn about earthworms (or whatever topic is on the agenda)." In this way, the expectation of learning about something in particular is established.

This expectation of learning about something is a two-way street. The student expects to be taught about the stated subject (earthworms, in this case) and the teacher expects the student to learn what she or he teaches about that subject. As children move up the grade levels, they are held increasingly accountable for learning the content of lessons and courses. Accountability is measured and recorded, usually through assignments and tests that are reviewed, rated, scored, or graded.

Even in the early (K-2) years of elementary school, children feel the presence of these formal learning—set curricular—expectations. In the beginning, in preschool and kindergarten, school expectations are usually felt in social more than academic areas. Children are expected to raise their hands, take turns, stay in line, sit still at circle time, restrict "bathroom talk" to the bathroom, and so on. In this way, they are eased into or acculturated to the school environment. School expectations build slowly, over time, through the years. Still, these formal school expectations, whether they are academic or social, can create a sense of pressure. The socialization pressure continues through childhood and adolescence (and likely some adult readers are feeling this pressure still now).

HELPING CHILDREN EXCEL AT FORMAL LEARNING

In the right form and dose, pressure is positive. Pressure contributes to, fuels, even can enhance, development. Some children respond to the pressure of the formal expectations of school with excellent work. They enjoy the challenge of meeting expectations. They seek the approval, the status, the attention, and the self-esteem that come from doing well.

Clearly stated expectations (and these are more frequently found at school than at home) require clearly defined responses from the children. "Draw a picture of this insect on this paper, using the brown felt pen" is a clearly stated expectation of the sort more commonly heard at school than at home. "Go do something quiet for a while" is not a clearly stated expectation, and more the sort heard at home than at school. That teachers are naturally more clear in their expectations is not surprising. Teachers are working in an environment that is more formally defined as a learning environment than is the home. And teachers have to measure the outcomes of their teaching: Were their teaching goals met? Were their desired outcomes actually met? How well? Why? Were the teachers clear enough with the students about academic expectations?

Most children appreciate the clarity of formal and explicit commands. ("Draw a picture of this.") This is because they want to understand precisely what they should do—are expected to do—and because they want to know that they are really expected to do it. The expectation is clear. There is no doubt in the child's mind about the requirement. This can be reassuring. (The opposite, vague, confusing expectations, can be quite unsettling.)

EXPECTATIONS 101

Children first learn about expectations at home, often in the form of rules. Parents can help children and teens succeed in school by helping them understand the what and why of expectations of behavior, boundaries, rules, and so on. This level of thinking about what is going on, why rules exist, why certain behaviors are expected, can help in the transition from home to school.

I must say more here—about another side of the expectation issue. Informal learning environments such as home can be loaded with potential for confusion and even failure. An unclear command such as "Go do *something* (anything?) quiet for a while," while allowing freedom of choice, leaves much room for failure to meet the expectation. The command is so vague that it raises a question about the need to comply (but *what* something? *how* long? do this *where*? and so on). And the command leaves questions regarding the path to approval. If one should comply, how would compliance look? After all, a child might go do something "quiet for a while" such as paint the furniture green or put a towel in the toilet and receive no approval at all.

A child who feels confident about her or his ability to figure out and to satisfy most informal expectations, and who enjoys a sense of success when satisfying these, can excel at the informal learning that can take place almost as a side effect of living in the home. It is also true that a child who feels confident about her or his ability to satisfy most formal expectations and who enjoys a sense of success when she or he does satisfy expectations can excel at formal learning. The linkage between these two forms of success (home success and school success) is important: Parents can give their children a head start on school success by making their expectations at least as clear and honest as those their children will find in school. This is true for children and teens of all ages. Here are some guidelines for clear expectations:

- Practice stating clearly and specifically what you want your child and or teen to do.

- Make certain that your expectations can be met. For example, do not expect a child in kindergarten to do advanced calculus. Do not expect an average ten-year-old to do quantum physics problems. You can teach complex skills and believe that learning these complex skills is indeed possible, but do not make demands unless they can be met. (Demands that cannot be met can be quite discouraging and even in some cases damaging, depending on how these demands and the expectations they are expressing are presented. Be sensitive to this side of the expectation process.)

- Be sure that you really mean it when you state an expectation.

- When your child meets the clearly stated expectation, give the child approval. Let the child know that she or he has met the specific expectation.

- If the child has tried, but has not entirely met your expectations because these expectations were too high, do not emphasize what has been done correctly and incorrectly. Focus instead on the fact that a genuine effort has been made to meet the expectation.

- Talk with your child or teen about expectations at home and at school. You might begin by talking about what an expectation is as soon as you feel your child can follow this conversation. Open dialogue about expectations—what they mean, how they are expressed, how it feels to be expected to do or be something, whether a particular expectation is working—can help adults and young people communicate. You will find that some children want more expectations placed on them, some want different expectations, some want expectations expressed differently, some want fewer expectations for various reasons. Talking openly about all this can help the adult refine and or revise or even take a break from the expectation process. There is no reason to be secretive about the expectation process, and there is no reason for a parent or teacher to be rigid about an expectation when it is not working.

- Take the understandings you gain to a new level: use these understandings to help ease the transition from home to school, and from school to home.

Some children are overwhelmed by the formal expectations made of them in the school environment. If your child is or may occasionally be one of these children, you can help your child discover that she or he is able to satisfy formal expectations. Using the above list, you can help your child practice at home. All children, regardless of their ages or personalities, benefit from parents' efforts to communicate their expectations clearly. Begin as early in the child's life as possible. And, if you have not started early, it is never too late. In fact, teens benefit immensely when expectations are very clear, when adults are very clear with them.

EASING THE TRANSITION

We cannot, except perhaps by remembering in detail the sensations we had during our own first school experiences, know how strikingly different the home environment is from the school environment. Even if a child is happy, proud, and thrilled to start school, a shock is experienced. By all outer appearances, most children seem to adapt, seem to overcome this shock, in an hour, a day, or a month. Yet, the shock is not gone—it is internalized. It is buried so deeply that we sometimes fail to continue to help ease the transition from home to school. This help is needed long after outer signs of shock disappear. It is needed even when no signs of shock appear. The critical transition from home to school continues through every day of the child's school year and school life, from day care and preschool right on through to elementary, middle, and high school. (In fact, many young adults experience such unrecognized transition shock even when going into college.)

So let's focus now on methods of easing the transition from home to school. These methods apply to the first entry into school (day care, nursery school, or preschool) in early childhood, the re-entry at the start of every school year (from preschool through twelfth grade), the event of moving to a new school or a new class within the same school, and yes, even to the transitions back into the school setting at the end of summer, winter, and spring vacations. These methods also apply to returns to school following doctor appointments, absences, and weekends. Above all, these methods of easing transition are an important part of the success of each school day:

- Always make explicit, officially recognize (perhaps even celebrate or note in some way), the beginning of a school year, semester, week and day. Do the same for returns to school after holidays and after absences. Do not leave the child to experience the transition and any feelings associated with it on her or his own, often not having words for it. This is one way the "I don't wanna go back to school" attitude begins and eventually ends up being repeated regularly. The child feels something about going back to school, can't quite label it or describe its complexity, and grabs the most ready description of it. So, help the child by labeling all the back-to-school transitions. Say, regularly, "Tomorrow (or today) is important—you go back to school."

• Establish little rituals that mark these transitions and then stick to them. For example, for many families, Sunday night marks the end of the weekend and the beginning of the school week. Adopt and stick to regular Sunday night rituals. These might include a long bath and hair washing; a family circle or family reading time; an organization of the child's schedule for the coming week; a phone call to grandparents; a review of all homework or subjects being studied.

• Put together a list of your Sunday back-to-school activities. Post it somewhere where the child can see it easily, even if the child does not yet read. Also establish school night rituals. These can include laying out of the next day's clothes; packing the school bag; making the lunch if one is required; collecting and putting into order any items, homework, papers, notes, going back to school. (Order is such a great help when one's life feels somewhat jumbled or at least in transition all the time.)

• For big transitions, such as those following a midyear or summer vacation, use a wall calendar posted where your child can see it. Mark the days off in one color and put a star or pleasant colored box around each first day of school after a vacation. The first day of a new school year should have its own special color or mark. If the child is old enough, have the child mark the calendar. Moving into adolescence, encourage the same practice, maybe moving to a more grown-up calendar, or even a date book. (In fact, this is a great opportunity for learning to use a paper or electronic datebook in addition to keeping a wall calendar.)

RESPECTING CHILDREN'S DIFFERENCES

Remember that, although children are quite predictable, each one has her or his own idiosyncrasies. Each child is different. Each child reacts to school differently at different times of the year, at different ages, in different family circumstances. Each child's special reaction evolves over time.

So many things affect a child's reaction to school. A parent cannot shelter a child from everything that might generate a minor but negative reaction to school. Instead, a parent must be as aware as possible of all influences on the particular child and the gravity of these influences on that child. Labeling these influences for the child and discussing them in a way that does not predict a negative effect is helpful, even important. Tell the child that you see that a disagreement with friends, or being sleepy during the day, or being hungry, or whatever it is, could be bothering her or him.

THE HOME LIFE BEHIND SCHOOL STRESS

School can be a stressful experience for a child. Before parents and teachers seek to tackle the sources of school stress, however, it is essential that they examine the home life of the child. When a child resists going to school, performs or behaves poorly at school, or has difficulty paying attention in class, the child could be bringing problematic elements of her or his home life to school.

One of the obvious places to start is with the amount of sleep the child gets. Examine your child's sleeping environment. Where is her or his bedroom in relation to the nearest street with vehicular traffic? Can you move this bedroom to a quieter part of your house or apartment? Consider placing heavy material over the windows at night (without blocking good ventilation, please). Is this bedroom near a noisy vibrating refrigerator? If so, this refrigerator can be turned down at night or you can put an automatic timer on it.

Examine the way your child organizes her or his time. Does she or he go to sleep early enough to wake up without an alarm? This is ideal, and naturally, given modern lifestyles, quite rare. However, do keep this model of natural rest cycles and times in mind. Look beyond calculating the amount of sleep (number of hours per night); see your child's general use of all time, whether awake, somewhat awake, sleeping, trying to sleep, trying to wake up. Is she or he often rushed in the morning? Does she or he have time for a satisfying breakfast? Plan your child's day so that that child can get what she or he needs while doing what must be done. No last minute rushing. It is possible to do this. Organize your child's time so that she or he spends it instead of it spending the child. Place a daily schedule on the wall. (You are the organizer of your child's time, aren't you? You do teach your child how it feels to organize and be moderately organized, don't you?)

Examine your child's eating habits. Does your child have at least a piece of fruit or juice to break the night-long fast in the morning? I say "at least" here because some children are not hungry very early in the morning. Pressuring these not yet hungry children to eat a hearty breakfast before school can, for some, start the day with psychological and, often, gastric stress. Whatever you do, do not give your child white sugar-loaded or sugar-covered foods or caffeinated tea and coffee. You wouldn't drive your car very far on bad fuel or on empty. Treat your child's body at least as well as you treat your vehicle. Cut out junk fuels such as caffeine and white sugar and give your child's body some real food. (Sugar-covered jelly doughnuts do not qualify as quality fuel.)

Examine your child's level of physical exercise. Teach your child a few gentle stretches to be done for a few minutes at the beginning and at the end of each day. (During the day is a good idea as well.) Gentle stretching can stimulate blood flow and reduces stress without causing strain. I emphasize *gentle* here, because anything more is not needed and should not be done unless the body has already been physically active in the time right before the stretching. Slow, calm, gentle and not forced stretching can soothe and calm a seemingly overactive child and can increase energy in a seemingly underactive child.

I say seemingly here, because what the child appears to be may or may not be what the child is. Do, however, watch your child's energy patterns. Does your child seem to you to be too quiet, or perhaps rather lazy, even sedentary? Or does your child seem to have the opposite condition, more energy than she or he knows what to do with? (And more than you know what to do with?) How much any of this (both the seeming underactivity and the seeming overactivity) reflects directly what is going on around the child—mimics it, or maybe exists in opposition to parents and siblings' energy patterns? Is this child's energetic patterning balancing what is taking place around the child? Or is something else such as nutrition, anxiety, or just being normal and moving through stages of development taking place?

If you are concerned, visit the child's doctor for a full checkup. Also, talk to your child's teacher for another perspective on your child's level of physical activity. Although many children are naturally physically active, some are not. Emotional problems, tiredness, improper nutrition, and even television addiction can lead to decreased or increased physical activity in a child. Build in structured physical activity such as a sport, or some dance or gymnastics classes. And do get out and play games like tag with your child. You can probably use the exercise yourself.

Examine your child's home life and social life. Does home feel like a safe place to go? Does your child have the opportunity to make deep and satisfying contact with each of your family members? How about friends? Does your child have ample opportunity to play or socialize with friends of about the same age? Does your child have a close friend, someone to share fun with? These are essential in a child's life.

If you live more than five minutes from school, examine your child's commuting activities. If you drive, try to use your commute time in a healthy way. The trips you and your child make to and from school are expenditures of valuable time. These minutes add up to hours and weeks. And the weeks turn into years. This is the time of your child's life (as well as of your own), so use it well. Find audiotapes or CDs that are fun or soothing to sing along or listen to. Try singing along together without music. Talk about fun or interesting topics. Be available if your child wants to talk about a personal problem; however, do not introduce painful topics or disciplinary actions on the way to or from school. Do not force conversation during these trips; volunteer it and respond to your child's openings. Try not to argue or fight on the way to school. Life is demanding enough for a developing child and or teen, and transition times are not the place to work through parent-child issues.

Look for other possible areas of stress outside of school. Make a game out of it. Be a detective. Investigate everything thoroughly. Come face to face with the sources of your child's stress. You may find that a parent or two parents under stress are primary sources. Many of your own stressors can be changed, just as your child's can. Many stressors can be made less stressful by simply eating, sleeping, and exercising regularly. Stressful lifestyles can be reorganized. As you reorganize your child's life, reorganize your own. You must commit to this reorganization of yourself as well as of your child for you and your child to feel the benefits. Keep repeating SEW: S for sleep, E for exercise, W for water. SEW a good life style for yourself and your child. Your child will share this with her or his child years from now. (You can eventually add an N for nutrition: SEWN.)

CHILDHOOD QUASI AND ACTUAL HYPOCHONDRIA

Sometimes, children fake or perhaps imagine, or even imagine into reality, illness to miss a day of school. Strangely enough, this happens even when home life is more stressful than school life. Because of its significance, let's focus for a moment on some critical aspects of childhood hypochondria. Note that standard definitions of hypochondria such as "imagined illness" say little about what is actually taking place. Full-on hypochondria in its actual state is a severe form of anxiety about one's health.

Children learn from adults, and in too many cases, children learn hypochondria and its tendencies from their environments. Adults can help by watching their own behaviors and what they are modeling for their children.

Children exposed to hypochondria-prone parents see parents exhibiting symptoms such as excessive fear of having a particular disease; excessive worry that minor symptoms mean there is a serious illness; an unusually high number of doctor visits and exams; unusually frequent instances of checking one's body for symptoms and problems and changes in vital signs; switching doctors and "doctor shopping" an unusual number of times; expression of a high degree of frustration with one's doctors and medical care; obsessive amount of research on health conditions; frequently thinking one has a disease after learning that such a disease exists; high degree of emotional distress around any of these activities; high degree of strain in emotional relationships around any of these activities; and even interference with normal life functions around any of the above.

The need for attention and care. A child exhibiting symptoms of physical illness may get more attention for her or his physical pain than she or he would get for emotional pain. When a deep need (and sometimes only a merely mild need) for attention and care is not being met—or the child does not feel as if it is being met—something like hypochondriacal symptoms may feel like the next best way to get what is desperately wanted.

The fostering of dependence by family members. Family members can inadvertently encourage hypochondriacal symptoms in a child by placing emphasis on physical problems above all other forms of expression and by responding more to physical illness than to other, less tangible experiences of family members.

The need to manipulate others. Feeling powerless in a family or social setting can lead some children to resort to physical symptoms. These symptoms can serve as a way to make requests for, and even demands on, parents and other caregivers for time and attention.

The desire for whatever advantages the "sick role" brings. Having discovered that the sick role brings control over others and draws attention, some children use this behavior again and again. Once this pattern is formed, it, like many other patterns, can be difficult to break.

A way to avoid the demands of life. It is not unusual to at least contemplate staying, if not actually be staying, home from school or even from work to avoid demands. This is a natural inclination. However, this behavior and its more extreme condition, unchecked hypochondria, can become a way of staying home from life to avoid its demands and responsibility. Work with this problem while your child is young. Be sensitive to your child's fears of what is out there in the world. Initiate, but do not force, discussions about fear and give your child the opportunity to hear you explain that everyone is afraid from time to time.

A response to difficulties of self-expression. When it is hard for a child to say what she or he is thinking or feeling, when a child has not learned outlets for emotions, the child tends to find outlets through her or his body.

A behavior learned from parents or relatives. Hypochondriacal behavior can run in families. Children tend to take on the behavioral styles of their parents or other relatives and then pass these on to their own children. Examine your own and other family members' behaviors to see if you or someone else is setting this type of example for your child.

Intensely experienced events. These may also contribute to the development of childhood (and adulthood) hypochondria. Grieving the death of a loved one or witnessing a death (even on television) can bring with it physical pain and even symptoms similar to those experienced by the person who died.

The experience of actual illness or injury. Children and teens tend to be preoccupied with their bodies. Illnesses and injuries can evoke strong responses and lasting memories, even when the injuries are minor ones.

The transition or expected transition back to school after a weekend, holiday, summer vacation, illness, or move can create all kinds of anxiety. Without parents acknowledging this anxiety in some way, a child is coping (or not coping) with that anxiety all alone.

Establish a continuing calm and close dialogue with the child, talking about life in general, a dialogue in which sometimes you both may talk about your mental and physical feelings and sensations. You can even play the game, What do I feel most about my body right now? Do not tell your child what to feel. Listen and reflect on what you hear. The dialogue itself may relieve some of the child's tension. Keep in mind that your child's mind and body are interconnected, as are your own. Mental biochemistry can create and regulate emotional pain. It can control physical pain. Emotional biochemistry can set physiological biochemistry into motion. Unpleasant feelings can cause sensations of sickness, just as sickness can cause unpleasant feelings. It works both ways. When your child has the flu, she or he can be grouchy, low in spirit. When your child is grouchy and low in spirit, she or he can develop nausea or a stomachache. The distinctions between mind and body are not so cut and dry.

Whatever the causes or symptoms, the transition from home to school is always felt to some degree. Although you cannot and should not solve all of your child's difficulties in life, you can be aware of the fact that children feel this transition. Just knowing that their parents understand that this is a transition, and that a transition can be unsettling, can help.

Lost in the World (Illustration by Angela Browne-Miller)

Part Three

That Thing We Call Home

CHAPTER **10**

The Child and Teen in the Family Environment

Then Cinderella said, "May I try, too?"

Her stepsisters rolled their eyes and said, "The slipper will never fit you!"

But the king's servant said that it was only right that she be allowed to try. So Cinderella stretched out her foot.

The stepsisters were surprised. The glass slipper fit Cinderella's foot so perfectly it might just as well have been made for her!

To their further amazement, Cinderella reached into her pocket and brought out the matching glass slipper.

At that moment, Cinderella's fairy godmother appeared, but only Cinderella could see her. With a wave of her magic wand, she turned Cinderella's rags into a gown even more beautiful than the one she had worn to the ball.

Her stepsisters then recognized Cinderella as the lovely princess from the ball. They knelt before her and apologized for treating her so badly. Then Cinderella, who was as kind as she was beautiful, said, "It's all right, sisters. I forgive you both."

Samantha Easton, *Cinderella*

Think of the family environment as the nest. This is the nurturing place in which the child's early survival and ongoing survival during childhood (including adolescence) are ensured. It is also the primary site in which the child's potential can be stimulated and even enhanced, or overlooked and even thwarted, as she or he grows from birth to adulthood. Parents seem to know this and are hungry for information about how to raise their children and teens well.

SUPERCHILD AND SUPERTEEN PRESSURE

Let's start with this thing, this idea, this phantom we call the superchild. It is not surprising that parents want to know how to help their children become superchildren, maximizing their potentials to the extreme. We see this in the superbaby preoccupation. However, superbabies are ideas that come from the same place as those superwomen and supermen ideas: the cabbage patch of the American dream as seen on television and in our imaginations. Wanting a child to be super-intelligent and super-accomplished by kindergarten is responding to competitive pressure. It is also asking a child to do what many an adult asks her or himself to do: Be a high achiever. Be invincible like a machine. The ideal machine is all powerful, flawless, perfect, and, in a word, super. We dream that we and our children have the capacity to function like these ideal machines (the likes of which we've never seen in real life because machines break down).

This superbaby fascination is a modern luxury. Until the beginning of the 20th century, physical survival was the primary objective of child rearing. This is because at that time over one in ten children died by the age of five. For most parents, the question was not one of rearing a child, but whether or not the child would survive to be reared at all. Parents today are indeed fortunate to have the largess to even dream of superbabies. When physical survival is at stake, intellectual training in early childhood is rarely seen as an issue.

We've also changed our perceptions of childhood. Children were once viewed as property, additional helping hands and sources of income. Families depended on their children to help them survive. Now it is rare for a child to contribute to the family income until the late teens, if at all. Early childhood is now viewed as being prime time in an individual's life. It is during this time that a human being's development can be most encouraged or most severely curtailed. In these early years, many modern parents see themselves as having the opportunity to produce and rear a superbaby: an individual who will grow into a superkid, a superchild, and a person who will excel in adulthood—excel in some way. This superchild pressure puts children and their parents under a great deal of stress and is perhaps best avoided or at least redefined.

The vision of the superchild: a person trained to be successful in a society based on competitive individualism. Does it pay off? Not necessarily. Do parents have to buy into it? No. What I suggest parents do instead is focus on the children's environments: Are these environments safe? Are these environments nurturing? Are these environments rich in stimulation?

The rich family environment is not about dollars and cents, money, in itself. Rich here means nurturing and stimulating of positive mental and moral development along many avenues. It is highly attentive to the individual developmental needs of each child. What this means is that as a child grows and changes, the family environment responds to her or his changing needs, both at home and at school.

THE SPECIAL ISSUE OF GROWTH AND DEVELOPMENT

Because developmental changes are most dynamic, rapid, and crucial during early childhood, considerable research on growth and development has focused on children under six, or preschool-age children. The units of time allotted in the definition of developmental periods are shortest for the earliest years of life, and these developmental units get longer as the child ages. Here is one calendar of child development as per school stage and age, which of course varies for each child:

Infancy (first year)
Newborn (birth through 28 days)
Early infancy (first 6 months)
Late infancy (7 through 12 months)
Toddlerhood (1 through 3 years)
Early toddler (1 to 1 1/2 years)
Terrible two's (1 1/2 to 2 1/2 years)
Trusting three's (2 1/2 to 3 1/2 years)
Preschool age (from 3 up to or through 5 years)
Early preschool (2 1/2 to 3 years)
Midrange preschool (3 to 4 years)
Late preschool (4 to 5 or sometimes 6 years)
Elementary school age (many ages grouped together ranging from 6 to 18 years)
Kindergarten age (around 4 to 6 years)
Lower elementary school age (around 5 through 8 years)
Upper elementary school age (around 9 through 11 years including latency age)
Middle school age (around 11 through 12 or 13 sometimes 14 years)

Junior high school or middle school (ongoing latency age and then tween-age years coming right before and on into early adolescence)

High school age (around 13 through 18 to 19 years)

Early high school (13 to 14 or 15)

Middle high school (14 to 15 or 16)

Higher high school (16 to 18 or 19)

However helpful such a list may seem, it does not say much about any one child's development. The ability to predict landmarks of what we call normal growth and development is of use, yes, but of limited use. Every individual develops at her or his own rate. Any time we fail to take into account a child's unique characteristics, we risk neglecting crucial responses to that child's own characteristics and needs. Familial care, care provided by the family and care provided by friends and relatives, is less apt to overgeneralize from one child to the next than is care and education in a group or school setting. This is primarily because there are fewer children in the home and the caregivers, especially the parents, have a greater stake in each of the children's individual development. After all, they are related to the child. They have a biological investment in the outcome of each individual childhood. (Schools and other settings for out-of-home care and education do care about the individual; their goals, however, are different: they are working toward the good of the group of students or children they serve.) Hence, the care a child receives at home is usually the most important in that child's life.

DEFENSE AGAINST INSTITUTIONS

Families can protect children from the necessary generalization and the frequent overgeneralization that society imposes on them. Overgeneralization can have detrimental effects on children. For example, a physically disabled child may be hindered in her or his development of academic competencies by a school's environmental inadequacies, by barriers such as the lack of easy wheelchair access to the computer room at school. When skills deemed normal for that child's age cannot be developed or stimulated or enhanced, alternative skills and other behaviors may emerge, sometimes precocious and other times more impeded than expected. The danger is that essential steps in that child's development may be missed or may occur but go unrecognized.

The comparison of any individual's development, whether or not she or he is considered to be disabled, to one normal curve can lead to a serious misdiagnosis of mental potential and ability. When a child who is not cognitively disabled fails to test well because of physical disability, emotional problems, or bilingual difficulties, then I.Q., achievement, and other types of academic tests used can lead educators to the wrong conclusions about that child.

Other problematic applications of the notion of so-called normal growth and development stages stem from a limited understanding of its concepts. The principles of growth and development are built on the concepts of: growth, which refers to change in physical size; maturation, which refers to the natural capacity of any individual to progress over time; learning, which refers to the process of acquiring new skills and knowledge; and development, which refers to any increase in competency owing to maturation or learning. Growth and development are thus the product of at least four of these processes, but these processes do not always occur together. Someone who is growing may not be learning. Someone who is growing old (in later life) may still be developing in some way, but will not be recognized as doing so because her or his changes are not interpreted as growth. And even in young people, the effects of simple maturation or just the passage of time may be interpreted as complex development when they are not. Although parents and teachers must be very aware of children's growth, maturation, learning, and developmental curves, they must constantly strive not to misinterpret or overgeneralize them.

COMPONENTS OF A RICH FAMILY ENVIRONMENT

The family environment defends children against, and prepares them for, the overgeneralization and institutionalization pressures they face in school and society. There are many components of this defense:

Love and other emotional contact. A child needs a place where feelings are openly and honestly acknowledged, where feelings are safely felt and expressed in a way a child can understand them. The family is the first line of defense against what can seem to many a child to be a confusing and impersonal world.

Let's say that all children are wonderful beings. Each and every one of them is born with tremendous potential. No one knows for certain what guarantees the realization of that potential, but love is a good bet. Although love is a vague and difficult feeling to describe in terms of precise activities, it is important for parents to be certain that they:

- Communicate "I love you" regularly in words and in actions.
- Offer, but do not force, physical affection—hugs and kisses are great communicators of love; Do not go more than a day or two without offering physical affection.

In emphasizing and seeking to express love, do not overlook other emotions. You can approve and disapprove of behaviors, but not feelings. All feelings are valid feelings, whether they seem positive or negative or neutral, whether they are felt by children or adults. Recognize and label (but do not judge) feelings for your children. Seek ways of allowing dialogue about feelings, even seemingly negative ones such as jealousy and anger. Communicate that it is all right to feel some jealousy or anger, that such feelings are worth understanding and discussing, but that it is not all right to say cruel things or to hit people or to break their things. Make this a consistent theme. Welcome expression of emotion in acceptable ways while consistently setting limits on unacceptable behaviors.

- Set aside special times for listening to each child's feelings with an open heart and a relatively closed mouth.
- Help the child develop a repertoire of behaviors that are acceptable and attach these behaviors to feelings: "When I am angry I . . . , but I do not. . . ."

AVOID STONY SILENCE

I have been describing the establishment of an environment of rich, ongoing, and healthy emotional expression for the child. The opposite childhood experience is provided by parents who use stony silence as their main way of maintaining control and of expressing or avoiding emotion. These parents create an invisible wall that no one can penetrate. Their children are cut off from emotional contact and, to survive, must learn to do without it. Imagine, hour after hour, day after day, week after week of cold silence coming from one or both of the two most important people in your life. This silence helps shape a child's personality by teaching detachment as a life script.

Emotional contact is an essential part of healthy human development. It is so essential that extreme lack of close contact in infancy can (but does not always of course) result in serious problems and even death. The type of emotional contact a child receives, especially in her or his early years, is an extremely influential part of that child's psychological development. This early emotional training creates lifelong patterns of relating. Whatever the age of the child, love and emotional contact can make a big difference in his life and mental development.

Comfort and security. Communicating to a child in a negative way is likely to lead to negative feelings and behavior. Threatening a child instills fear.

Saying "I am ashamed of you" instills shame and guilt. Asking "What is wrong with you?" instills a sense of incompetence, a feeling that something is, indeed, wrong. Don't we all know adults with these traits—negative feelings, fear, shame, guilt, a sense of incompetence?

Of course there will be times when you raise your voice with your children. Your children are not saints and neither are you. (Anyway, who is to say that saints never raise their voices?) Keep in mind, however, that some of what you say emphatically and loudly can be taken from the list of positive, optimistic messages that follow. All too often we tend to be dramatic in our expressions of disappointment, anger, and negativity and too quiet in our expressions of approval, love, and positivity.

Optimism. Consider giving your child positive and optimistic messages about her- or himself. These messages are some of the building blocks of a happy life. Try communicating some of these messages to your child:

- You are wonderful.
- I like you.
- Thank you for being with me, for being in my life.
- You may live a long life, and do it happily.
- You are a satisfied person.
- Add to this list some of the words of approval or affection that you would like to have heard (or did hear) on a regular basis when you were young and practice saying these words to your child daily.

Clear communication. One of the most disturbing types of human interaction is unclear communication. Although we are all troubled by vague and sometimes mixed messages, children suffer more with these than do the rest of us. Why? Because children are the least likely to say to themselves or to someone else, "That is not clear; I am uncertain as to what is meant by that." Children are frequently deciphering adults' communications, guessing as to what is actually meant or really wanted, and adults should keep this in mind. At the same time they are guessing at what adults really mean, children are trying to please these adults, seeking to either receive love in return or to avoid punishment.

You can help your child by editing your comments on an ongoing basis. Of course, we don't always have the presence of mind to think before we speak. But you can listen to what you say to your child as you are saying it. If the message is not simple and crystal clear, repeat it until you have gotten it right and then repeat the refined statement a few times in a row.

For example, a parent might say, "Johnny, it's 5 o'clock and I told you to have your room and hands and face clean before dinner and you haven't. So go to your room and do it." This is a lot of message in one statement. The tone in which all of this is spoken is the dominant message: Is the parent angry, disappointed, or simply matter-of-fact? The clarity or lack of clarity is another critical piece of the message: When is dinner? Does the child still have time? How can the child actually obey right now—how can he wash his hands and face while he is in his room?

This message must be cleaned up. First of all, if the parent is angry or disappointed, the parent should say so. Try, "I am angry because you have not done what I asked you to do." Identify the specific emotion and then the actual message—if there is one, as too often adults are just angry for no particular reason and this confuses children and teens. Do not leave a child the job of trying to interpret a parent's tone of voice. All too often parents combine their own stress and exhaustion with irritation and the need to discipline their children. This is quite normal, but children (of all ages) should be helped to know what emotional elements are present in the voice: "I am also very tired, I had a hard day at work."

Second, directions must be clear, very clear. "Go to your room and do" exactly what? How long? Who will say when it is done? Be careful not to give directions that are impossible to follow correctly if followed verbatim, word-for-word. Avoid mixed messages and crazy-making no way out double binds (you are wrong if you do this but also wrong if you do that). Listen to yourself. Are you telling the child that she or he is wrong either way? "You didn't do what I asked you to do and it's too late to do it now." What is the child to do? Why bother saying this?

Healthy camaraderie and social interaction. No family life is entirely harmonious. No family can avoid tension and disagreement all the time. But every family can aim for as much healthy companionship as possible.

- Create an atmosphere of being on each other's team. Root for your children, cheer them on. Have them root for each other and their parents as well.

- Sit together and enjoy each other. Say that this is what you are doing, that you are spending some time together and enjoying each other, so that children can define the experience.

- Teach your children, by example, to say "hello" and "goodbye," and to look for positive things to say about family members. Encourage positive statements: "Mom, I like your dress." "Cathy, you look pretty today." "You are reading so well now, I'm proud of you." "You did a great job." No need to make things up. We can all see something positive in someone else if we learn to look for it.

Interdependence. Need each other. Although overdependence can become a problem when it is encouraged, nurtured, or expected, interdependence is healthy. Family members do need each other. Make this clear. "I need some help getting dinner ready." "I need to talk about my day." "I need someone to tell me if my hair looks O.K. from the back."

Identification. Children identify with their families, no matter how extended or how small. Even if you are a single parent of one child, you can build a family consciousness into your child's life. "We are the Smith family," or, if there are two parents in the family using different last names, "We are the Haskin-Smith family." Create a family slogan or song or banner. Establish family traditions. Family identity helps children feel that they have roots, that they have a place on this planet.

Opportunity for responsibility. As I noted earlier, it was not very long ago in history that children were considered chattel, the property of their parents, primarily of their fathers. The birth of an able-bodied child, especially a male baby, was looked on as the arrival of two additional wage-earning hands for laboring both at home and at work. Before the enactment of child labor laws, even working class children of what we now call "beginning school age" were put to work for long hours in guilds, factories, and mines.

Quite rightly, we now protect children from such exploitation. Instead, we allow them a childhood. We provide them with formal education. We take care of them in ways unheard of two centuries ago. Yet, in an almost subconscious effort to protect childhood from even the faintest hint of exploitation and from the neglect and abuse associated with it, we sometimes stumble into another form of neglect and of abuse through neglect. This is the neglect to teach responsibility through chores and participation in the family work.

Why is this form of neglect abusive? Because it creates children who know little about the level of effort or even the type of effort that goes into creating their physical realities. Others work hard to serve a child: to feed, clothe, drive to school and lessons, pay the rent, and maintain the household. Parents are unsung heroes. But even unsung heroes can neglect to share the responsibility for household chores with their children.

Children who grow up with little participation in the responsibility of maintaining a home and a family are missing out in several ways: They do not learn the essential how-to's of living. They do not feel the pride of contribution. They do not learn responsibility. They do not learn some very practical and essential skills. They grow up expecting to be taken care of. This last one is a dangerous expectation, one that affects children's school performance. Children expecting to be taken care of do not just drop such expectations in school. They may not request that their teachers baby them, but they often show much less initiative then children who have some sense that they can take care of themselves. Children who do not share in the job of running their households do not develop certain aspects of motivation, self-esteem, and initiative. In school, they may not raise their hands with questions as often, or use a dictionary on their own as often as more resourceful children.

Provide your children opportunities to become resourceful, give them responsibilities. This can have a great effect on their intellectual development. Simple, age-appropriate tasks or chores that can be successfully completed by the child are quite valuable. Successful completion of tasks generates a sense of competence, a feeling of purpose, a sense of importance. In the completing of simple tasks, a child learns that even the most basic projects have beginnings, middles, and ends. The child learns to value following through and assuming responsibility, taking initiative. This learning transfers to other parts of life. The sense of competence and the taking of initiative are essential elements of school success.

Reward systems. Positive behaviors must be rewarded. The reward can be a hug, a positive statement, the awarding of a privilege or something material. Match the reward to the behavior being rewarded, by degree and by your ability to keep providing the reward. Be careful with monetary rewards. Over time, money provided for every achievement will become expensive and will create a false expectation that life will consistently pay one for doing good things.

Play. Play a lot. This is easy to say, but play what? How? Alone or with others? Play serves two basic functions. The first is what is described as the assimilative function. As an assimilative function, play is a social activity that helps a child integrate into the society. This is, basically, play with another child or other children in which the children interact. Play also serves an autogenetic function. As an autogenetic function, play is a personal activity that is associated more with individual needs than with those of a social group or society. A child can do this type of play alone or with others, but its developmental effects are more personal than social.

These forms of play need not be mutually exclusive. If play serves both a social or public (assimilative) and an individual or personal (autogenic) purpose, developmentally oriented play will encourage both. Because individualization is as much a part of acquiring a social identity as is socialization, play that addresses either of these is, in the end, a social activity. A parent, caregiver, or teacher can encourage both lines of development by providing opportunities for structured and unstructured play.

Given that play takes various forms and serves various purposes, parents do best to encourage many different types of play. Have your children play alone, with friends, and, just as important, with you. Encourage structured group play in which games or activities are clearly defined (hide and seek, four-square, cards, basketball). Encourage unstructured group activity in which two or more children must deal with each other within a minimum of adult guidance. Encourage quiet reading time and play-alone time, in which a child goes inside her or his own mind for entertainment and stimulation. (This is something like playing dolls or trucks or drawing, not watching television.)

Ritual. Ritual is a special type of structured activity that often incorporates recreation; however, it involves much more than play. Rituals include daily patterns such as meals and bedtimes, arrivals and departures, and celebrations such as birthdays and holidays. The importance of ritual in a child's development is twofold. First, it gives the child a sense of social patterns—meals occur regularly, naptime is at the same time each day; these are activities that people have in common. Second, rituals, when they are regular observations of special holidays, serve to familiarize the developing child with her or his own culture or subculture, encouraging identification and socialization.

Direct moral judgment. Rules and codes of behavior are guidelines for the development of moral judgment. These guidelines motivate children to stay within them and to acquire socially acceptable patterns of behavior. The motivation I speak of here is a combination of enforcement (disciplinary action) and reinforcement (approval and affection). As a child matures, morality and moral reasoning grow through a developmental sequence. The earliest stage of moral judgment responds to traditional authoritarian control. The later stages of moral judgment depend on an ability to comprehend the reasons behind the rules. Parent and teachers, therefore, assist the development of moral judgment in a child by teaching not only the rules but also the reasons for the rules. The more your child must evaluate her or his own behavior in terms of social and family rules, the more your child must practice moral thinking—and thinking in general.

Developmental abilities. Daily life offers every member of the family challenges that inspire development. Look for these opportunities for your children. Putting objects away, matching spoons with spoons, blocks with blocks, nuts with nuts, and bolts with bolts are wonderful exercises for a child. These exercises require that a child organize her or his thoughts. Even though the work is with physical objects, as it is being done, mental concepts, ideas, are being mentally manipulated. Look for opportunities in daily life to stimulate your child's mental organization processes. If you are trying to sort paper clips by size, ask your child to help you do so. You can find exercises of this type for children of all ages. Your teenager can help you organize your receipts at tax time. Your ten-year-old can help file your papers. Your seven-year-old can separate unlabeled flower bulbs by type, color, and size.

INTENTIONAL DEVELOPMENT

Beyond the above activities, many of which unfold naturally in daily life, there are many more formal opportunities for the stimulation of your child's development. You can plan regular educational activities for your child, including:

- counting and solving mathematical problems together
- doing puzzles
- building models and engines;
- visiting museums, nature preserves, and so on
- taking up an educational hobby such as rock or bug collecting
- enrolling in acting, gymnastics, aikido, dance, or music lessons

By building specific educational activities into a child's life, beginning at a young age, these activities become an unquestioned, natural part of life. By the time the child is ready to pick and choose her or his own lessons and other educational activities, the child should be used to the fact that such activities are a part of life and that the decision is which educational activities should be engaged in rather than whether or not to engage in any. I have found the early start especially helpful when it comes to dance and music lessons.

Family music. Family music can be mentally, culturally, and spiritually stimulating. If you play an instrument, do so for and with your child. If you do not, try learning to play. Take music lessons as you have your child do the same.

Reading aloud. Never miss an opportunity to read *to each other*. I emphasize to each other here because, as early as possible, have the child share in the reading. Begin by having the child repeat phrases or sentences that you have just read aloud. Then have the child read the easy words in the sentence, pausing and pointing at the easy word each time you come to an "I" or a "the" or an "a" or any word you are reasonably certain that your child knows. Eventually, your child will share the role of family reader—the job of reading aloud. Many parents are thrilled when they realize that their children can read *them* to sleep.

Reading and working quietly together. Institute family quiet times during which all or most members of the immediate family sit in the same area of the house and read, sew, study, draw, or do activities requiring quiet concentration. This model is a behavior that your children will continue through their school years and into their adult lives. Too many modern families have replaced this type of family time with family television watching. Group television watching is an entirely different type of activity from that which I suggest here. It requires less concentration, less spiritual synergy, less togetherness. The physical bodies may sit closely but the hearts and minds tend to go blank, to be much less accessible then when each is reading her or his own book or sewing or drawing nearby. Television watching literally has a different biochemistry.

Role playing. Good family time is not always quiet. Try role playing. This provides a great opportunity for theatrical and emotional engagement. Have each family member play the role of someone else in the family. You may want to delegate these roles carefully if you have two or more children who are passing through stages of teasing each other. Perhaps they should not play each other, or perhaps they should but only with previously stated rules.

Other activities. Develop your own stimulating family activities. As you become increasingly sensitive to children's needs to identify with their families, and to see good uses of time modeled by their family members, you will discover your own ways of meeting these needs.

COUNTERINTELLIGENCE IN THE FAMILY

Although families can do a great deal to enhance the development of the mental abilities of their children, they can also detract from or discourage their children's mental abilities. We tend to overlook the many discouragements to intellectual thinking that are present in our children's lives. I will describe just a few of these here.

Family disorganization. Family disorganization is a form of counterintelligence. This is a family management issue. If your family life feels disorganized, do not assume that something is wrong with you or your family. You are sharing an experience with millions of modern families, most of whom need training in family management.

Family management is a psychological as well as a practical problem. The psychological state of parents is affected by the ease with which they feel they can manage their family lives and vice versa. When both parents work away from the home full time, they require advanced family management skills so that they can sanely and effectively meet the doubled demands of parenting and of working for pay. When neither parent has a spouse (or grandparent or employee perhaps) at home who serves as full time homemaker and family manager, effective management is all the more the key.

Although the economic status of a family determines its ability to afford a wide range of consumer goods and services, it says little about the family's ability to organize its time and energy. Scheduling and planning are challenges for most families, regardless of income. A family's ability to arrange time to shop, to commute, to be involved in community activities, to know the next-door neighbors, to prepare meals and to eat them, and, most important, to be together, are products of good family management.

Without time for it, parents do very little parenting, people do very little caring. Too many working parents live in a perpetual time crunch in which home serves as a station for sleeping, eating, paying bills, and changing clothes. When relationships between family members are caught in this crunch, people who actually love each other and care very much about each other start to grind away. It seems that many people find it is easier to be distant or irritable on the fly than to express good feeling in passing. Scheduling time for good feeling, as whimsical as it may sound, is essential. Somehow, too many of us made it into adulthood without learning to make and stick to workable family plans. We must show our children that it is possible to have time to be a family and to feel like one.

Family management can be difficult for working parents (both male and female working parents). Many working parents find that there are male-female differences in the way parents divide their time between work and home care (chores) and children (care of the children—child care). Many working parents have found that employed, married female parents average as many hours a week at work as do their male parent counterparts, but average more time on chores and child care. However, this profile is changing. Working male parents are increasing their time on home chores and child care each week. We have to wonder—how much "free" time do working parents of either sex really have? When free time is so limited, only careful planning creates time for the family—and maybe for the self.

And then there are the working single parents, both male and female, who frequently have to balance work and home and children all on their own. This very special working single parent balancing act is a feat of patience, endurance, commitment, necessity, and, of course, love.

PLAN TO DO SO

What this boils down to is a message from me, the author, to you: The only way to incorporate the suggestions I offer in this book into your children's lives and their mental developments, is to plan to do so. Write a weekly schedule that includes the suggestions in this and other chapters. Create a family reading time if you do not have one. Create official study times if they do not exist. Plan times to work with your children on the concentrated aspects of mental development I offer in Chapters 13 through 18. Select items from the other chapters that you want to emphasize and schedule them in to your lives. Many parents use an appointment book, kept in the communal living area, in which they write these activities. Write your family schedule your own way, but do it. Older children can help or even take charge of the planning. Fight the counterintelligence of family disorganization.

SIBLING ORDER ISSUES

Here is another, very different form of what I call counterintelligence in the family. Parents of more than one child cannot help but compare their children. Quite often, parents observe differences in mental ability, frequently noting that it is the firstborn child who seems a bit better adjusted to school. They often ask, Why does my first child seem brighter and better in school than my second child? Have I failed my second child or are first children naturally better at things? Is there anything I can do for my second-born? (Whenever I say "secondborn" here, I am referring to any child who was born after another sibling. This could be a third-, fourth-, or fifthborn as well.)

Whether or not we find our firstborns to seem brighter, many of us fall into a few very uncomfortable cultural traps. The first trap is the use of the word "better" in describing our children. Thinking in terms of "better" and "worse" oversimplifies people. Whenever we compare two people in a simple way, one will come out seeming to be more or less of something than the other. People are not simple beings. They cannot be compared simply. And children are people, too.

The second trap is one in which being brighter and more successful is equated with being better. Break this equation by dropping the emphasis on better. Being brighter and more successful does not necessarily have anything to do with being better. Many bright and successful people are better at some things and worse at others. Let go of this connection.

When it is the firstborn who seems to lead intellectually, we must be aware of the difficulty experienced by the second and later-born children. Firstborn children tend to be hard acts to follow for their younger siblings. "Sib order," the order in which children are born into a family, has a profound influence on children's perceptions of themselves. Firstborns tend to feel more confident and in control. And, quite often, but definitely not always, firstborn children are higher achievers in school and exhibit more leadership characteristics than do secondborn children. When they do so, firstborns then tend to carry these childhood characteristics on into adulthood, achieving and leading in adult life.

This is not to say that secondborn children do not do well in life. In many of the cases where there has appeared to be a gap between siblings' developments, secondborns (and other order-borns—thirdborns and so on) catch up to their firstborn brothers and sisters as they differentiate from them. Parents can encourage this differentiation process by creating opportunities for secondborn children to develop in areas in which the firstborn children are not actively involved. Sisters and brothers need not compete to be better than each other. They can enjoy their differences.

All too often, secondborn children are expected to follow in the footsteps of firstborn children. Sometimes secondborn children intentionally or even unintentionally rebel. They develop a new role for themselves. As one secondborn explained, "My brother was always the best kid in the family and the best at school. So the only way I could be different was to be very bad and very stupid. He got all the positive attention—so I took what was left."

Every family is different and, therefore, every secondborn has a different experience. Sometimes the firstborn gets into a lot of trouble and the secondborn is able to differentiate by being the "good kid."

Another way families differ is in the age differences between their children. The more years between children, the greater the probability that each will have the firstborn type of experience. Children who are seven years or more apart will rarely if ever view themselves as occupying the same developmental territory. They thus compete less directly with their siblings.

Generally speaking, parents' direct influence on firstborns is greater than on the secondborns. Because they have only one child to parent at the beginning of the firstborn's life, their parenting energy is enthusiastic and undivided. Parents' expectations and desires for the success of their first-borns are more clearly transmitted. Firstborns tend to take in, to internalize, the level of drive and ambition that their parents have for them. They may also internalize any pressure to achieve that they feel. When the second child comes on the scene, parents' attentions are divided and may feel somewhat strained. Parental drive and ambition may have already been passed on to the firstborn. Something else may get expressed to the secondborn. The message, no matter how hard parents may try to avoid sending it, is often heard by the secondborn as "fit in to this already established family, take your place in line."

Parents are right to be concerned that their secondborns get second best. Yet, parents need not view themselves as failing their secondborns. It is important to make it clear that your parental love and optimism is not merit-based. Children who are not high achievers, **_whatever their birth order_**, need as much parental love and support as children who are achievers. Children who are not high achievers also need to feel that their parents are as optimistic about their futures as they are about the futures of high achievers.

Parents must also be sensitive to the effect that a firstborn's dominance due to seniority has upon the secondborn. Secondborns can be as strongly affected by seeming disapproval coming from firstborns as they are by what they may perceive is disapproval coming from their parents. Secondborns may feel they are having less importance in the family, less parental love and support, than the older sibling. (Whether this is actually taking place is another matter.) The firstborn has one or two loving parents all to her or himself for a while. The secondborn has one or two loving parents that she or he must share, and a sibling who is not necessarily loving (although of course many siblings are indeed loving with each other). This situation can interfere with mental, moral, emotional, and even physical development.

Watch sibling relationships closely. Brothers' and sisters' behaviors can in some cases be much more damaging to children than their parents' behaviors. Do not force your secondborn on your firstborn or vice versa. Let the children find each other when they are ready. Parenting is a question of balance. Parents are jugglers. Professional circus jugglers will tell you just how important timing is.

Credit yourself for the good things that you do for your children and that they do for themselves. Give yourself and each of your children approval aimed specifically at their own individual qualities on a regular basis. Approval is a great vitamin. It nourishes the soul.

TELEVISION

Here is the ultimate in counterintelligence when used in excess: Television, that electronic babysitter, permanent house guest, technological hybrid in-law. So many parents ask: Why do our children beg us for television as if it were water in a drought-parched desert? Why do our children become oblivious to all around them, even their favorite toys and loving parents, when it is on? What is it about that dull glow that attracts them so, even when the sun is most brilliantly lighting the world outside?

Television is *easy*. Even a child can turn it on, change the channel, and turn it off. Television is not *demanding*. A child can sit there, as numb as she or he pleases, and be entertained. There is no absolute demand that the young (or older) viewer think at all, even when the program being watched purports itself to be educational or, in newer buzz word terms, interactive. Television is *very present*. Parents can become dull with fatigue, get distracted by responsibility, be called to telephones, but television never gets exhausted or busy or called away. Television is always there with the flick of the switch. Television is *entertaining*. Even when the content is not entirely exciting, there is the color, the noise, and the perpetual motion. This sure beats parents—they can be dull, sit still, look tired and pale, and have little to say sometimes.

Television is a *passive stimulus*. No interaction, no bridge toll, is necessary. Do some children crave passive stimulation—something for nothing so to speak? Are most children stimulus junkies? Have we addicted the next generation to an electronic breast? Have we adults led the way for our children with our own television viewing behavior? Television is on at least six hours a day in the typical American household.

Yet, before we take our televisions to the garage and bash them to bits, we must remember that excessive use of almost anything is unhealthy. Television, in moderation and with guidance, can actually be a valuable addition to a child's life. I am, therefore, an advocate of controlled use of television. Television should be a supplement to life, not a substitute for it, and not a babysitter or best friend.

By "controlled use" I mean nonaddicted use—not uncontrolled, unlimited, unhealthy use, and not use to the exclusion of other important development activities such as being with the family, and reading, drawing, playing, exercising, helping around the house, and doing homework well instead of racing through it to get television time.

What might this controlled use of television look like? Parents must guide this use:

- Communicate (from birth, if you still have time to start this early, and from as early as you can in childhood otherwise) that television is a restricted activity, something determined by the parent. The earlier you begin implanting this concept in the child's mind, the easier it will be to maintain it as the child grows.

- Restrict television watching to a consistent number of hours a week. For school-age children, I suggest no more than ten hours a week (less is preferable), with over an hour of television viewing occurring only on days when there is no school. Preschool-age children have slightly different needs. Studies have shown that a certain amount of television viewing can actually be developmentally stimulating for preschool-age children, but after about ten hours per week, the effects of television viewing wane and become negative. What this means is that a little television can be good and a little more is less good and a lot more is bad. I found that my daughter's television watching, in the face of the explicit limits I am listing here, averaged six hours a week (including videos) during school weeks and eight hours when school was out. I stress averages here because I found that visits to friends' houses increased the weekly total. I also tried to find subtle ways of sticking to or coming in below the desired average by creating activities that left no time for television.

- Include videotape/DVD watching and educational television within the total hours. It is, after all, an image coming through the television screen. This holds for educational videos as well.

- Remember to maintain control over the type of program being watched. This holds for children of all ages. Cartoons, no matter how socially valuable or educational, should be limited. Try to avoid programming with commercials. Commercials are a brainwashing process, planting a "buy me" demand in the minds of children. Commercials are a poor use of your child's brain time. Educational programs such as nature, science, mathematics, geography, history, painting, and even cooking programs are wonderful, even for young children who may not understand all of what they hear.

- Restrict parental watching to evenings past bedtime or a room away from the central part of the house. Parents need not follow the same rules as children: parents' brains are past the extremely vulnerable stage. I nevertheless believe that many adults dull their minds with television overuse. A parent with a television-deadened mind cannot be intellectually stimulating to a child.

AN IMPORTANT NOTE REGARDING INTERNET AND ONLINE GAMING EXPOSURE AMONG YOUTHS

Almost daily exciting new technologies are emerging. We live in a wonderful era in which science and technology has made a great deal of technical learning available to many persons who would not otherwise access as much of this learning. Nevertheless, these new frontiers and increases in access bring with them hazards if we are not paying attention.

Television watching has primed our young people for screen watching and fixations on electronic media, which means that Internet viewing and text messaging, and other screen and electronic activities must be monitored by parents and teachers. Strict supervision of access to, and use of, the Internet and all electronic gaming and viewing activity is essential. These can be virtually (or even actually) as addicting as television.

Too many children and teens are exposed, right in their own homes as well as outside their homes, to Internet gambling, gaming, and pornography. The extent of this exposure is vast and already worldwide. Do not think your children and teens are immune to such exposure. Instead be aware of what forms of electronic and Internet media your children and teens are being exposed to. Know that purposefully and also negligently allowing a child to be exposed to pornography is considered a form of child abuse.

The child is in the family environment for a significant amount of her or his lifetime. Parents can make this environment stimulating or dulling, secure or threatening, safe or dangerous. Parents, you are in charge here.

CHAPTER 11

A Note about Child Witness Fallout

Seeing my daddy and mommy hit each other makes me shiver.
I hide when they start, 'cuz I don't wanna watch.
I hide when they start because I'm afraid.
Sometimes my dad comes and hits me too. Then he hits my mom when she tries to make him stop.
Thinking about it makes me want to kill someone or myself.
I grew up watching my dad beat on my mom. I hate her for taking it. I hate myself for not stopping it.
I am afraid if I get together with someone it will be the same way it was for my parents.
Not me, I'll never be like either of them!

> children and teens from homes with domestic violence

THE UNADDRESSED INJURIES

Volumes can be written about the effect of domestic violence, also called intimate partner violence, on children who witness it, feel to blame for it, may find role-modeling in it, and, when caught in the fray, are hurt emotionally as well as physically. Yet, there are countless emotional as well as physical injuries that children witnessing domestic violence (whether or not it is physical or emotional or financial or other) experience. And too many of these injuries are never recognized let alone addressed—not during childhood and not later during adulthood.

CARRIERS OF PATTERNS

Our children are the carriers into the future of our values and knowledge. They will most likely (and fortunately) want to improve on their parents' (yes, our) values and expression of these, and this is good! So much can be done better. These precious people, their parents' offspring, deserve a great deal of caring and intelligent assistance identifying, and recovering from, any exposure they may have had to adults' intimate partner abuse and violence—and their parents' pain around this abuse and violence. To break the cycle of intimate partner abuse and violence, as well as its long-term health and mental health effects, pain, and trauma, we must understand that all of this can spill from generation to generation in some form—unless a conscious and visible effort to stop the violence is made!

It is also important to see that when adults repeat patterns of emotional and physical violence and abuse around children, they are including children in these patterns. Any detrimental behavioral habits, addictions to negative behaviors, played out around children bring these children right into these patterns. Compulsive, destructive, abusive cycles of intimate partners include any children on the seeming sidelines. They cannot be unaffected. Nor can be they saved from the emotional roller coaster rides of cycles played out by adults who are likely, in some difficult-to-explain (to a parent let alone the child) way, addicted to the patterns they have established. No matter how much a parent believes a child is insulated from that parent's ongoing involvement in intimate partner violence and abuse, there is little protection from this reality for the child. Children see and hear—*and feel*—even the smallest signs of this problem.

TEACHING DENIAL

To pretend to children and teens that there is no abuse and violence taking place when there is is not only absurd but cruel. The young people do perceive something, they feel it, and usually also hear and see it or the injuries. When this feeling, hearing, and seeing is not validated by the parent, this denial of the actual reality is disturbing, confusing, and distressing. Why drive a child into denial-like patterns, teaching that denial of a serious problem is alright? Why add to a child's pain and roller coaster experience this sort of lesson in denial?

HARSH AND PAINFUL REALITY

The harsh and painful reality is that these children are dependent on these adults who are abusing and being abused. They have no way of ending the relationship with these adults, and they have no way of choosing not to need these adults. This dependence on these troubled adults, coupled with the mixed messages that children in these situations typically receive (such as it is wrong to hit people even though you see this happening here at home), can be highly stressful and emotionally disturbing for these children.

Riding the roller coaster of fight, feel better, fight, feel better, fight, feel better, and so on, children absorb elements of abuse and violence cycle patterning. Moreover, they absorb the ride itself—emotional high low, high low, high low, again and again. For some children, especially those who do not know what patterning is, or what is happening to them as witnesses of this abuse, these patterns can become deeply buried inside them. Many years later, or maybe not so much later, a trigger may fire the pattern into action, and the child is at risk of continuing the cycle of abuse and violence from generation to generation. Or the child is at risk of playing out the cycle of abuse and violence in another way, such as through alcohol, drug, or food addiction or other detrimental and dangerous behavioral patterns.

CHILDREN HAVE A RIGHT TO THIS INFORMATION

Children have a right to know what the risks of being child witnesses might be. We do not mind children seeking information about any family tree disease that they are at risk for, do we? Why would we mind children seeking information about the possible future abuse and violence they are at risk of being both the victims of and the sources of? And how dare we not inform children that the detrimental behavioral patterning they have witnessed may in itself be addictive—with these high low high lows—whether played out in the same form or another?

Children have a right to know what the long-term physical health and mental health effects of being child witnesses may be. Children exposed to domestic, intimate partner, abuse and violence are at a higher risk for a number of long-term health and social conditions not limited to being at risk of coming into adulthood playing out perpetrator and or victim roles. And we are still learning about the long-term effects of this violence on children. Or maybe we know more than we want to, with the signs all around us in this violent world where adults resort to violence as a means of addressing conflict.

These children should be told and taught early what it means to see a behavioral cycle, to see addictive behavior, to look closely and see the steps in troubled relating that can be changed, redirected, once these are identified—to slow down and *go conscious*!!!

Adults seeking to rewrite the programming they may have instilled in their children (when they allowed their children to witness emotional and physical violence) must teach their children the same thing they themselves need to learn: *how to recognize and change patterns of abuse and violence*. Not to teach these children these things out of concern that the material that will be taught is too much for children's ears and eyes is illogical. These children have already been exposed to intimate partner violence and abuse. Now they have a right to recapture this information in a way that prepares them to avoid the same experiences their parents have had. The material in this book, for example, is material young people can learn and many indeed have a hunger for. Young adults forming young intimate partner relationships are especially in need of this sort of information. Knowing how relationships work, knowing how to spot compromises and trades as they are being made, knowing the slippery definitions of intent and consent, is very important.

LOVE

Children want to see healthy love relationships. This provides a model for what good is possible, and for the roles they are likely to someday assume for themselves. Parents who allow atmospheres of emotional and physical abuse and violence in their homes are allowing the transmission of the message that it is okay to abuse someone you love; it is okay to be abused by someone you love; and it is okay to abuse yourself. However, this is not okay and that it is okay must not be taught.

Additionally, parents are modeling ways of loving, or ways of thinking one is loving, oneself and one's significant other. Children see this modeling and incorporate it into their world views, forming a deep level of unresolved confusion and disillusionment. How can love hurt so much? Is this the way it is supposed to be? Is this the self-respect my parents have for themselves? Is this low level of self-esteem all that one should try for? Children and teens are also faced with identity questions: Is all this abuse and violence because of me? What kind of person am I if I have caused this? Am I doomed to be just like my mother or father? If these are my role models, will I be able to learn any other better behavior? How do I know?

Being a child witness means watching two people who purportedly love each other act as if they hate each other, or two people—who want themselves or others to think there is love there—have and hurt each other. In a child's eyes, this does not compute. The messages are mixed, and are stored in the young mind mixed. The job of overcoming the mislabeling of acts of abuse and violence as love, and the related confusion, begins immediately in the young mind whose tolerance for intimate partner violence is already being programmed in, whether the child or anyone watching knows this.

PREVENTING AND ADDRESSING ALIENATION

Everything possible must be done to prevent young people from becoming alienated from themselves, their siblings, their parents, their lives in general. When the confusion, pressure or pain of a situation is too intense for a young person (or adult), this person may distance, detach, or respond to this situation in another manner. Parents and teachers must watch for signs of alienation, without blindly blaming each other for this alienation. Connect with the alienated young person; help that person outwardly express any confusion, emotional pain or pressure in healthy ways rather than in hurting oneself or others. Keep any adults' personal agendas in the background. There are many causes of alienation; all too often this condition is dangerously oversimplified. A multitude of factors (normal development, troubled development, hormonal changes, exposure to troubling media, abuse, etc.) can spur on such alienation; only some factors are obvious on the surface.

Clearly parents can play a role in fueling symptoms of alienation in their children. However, symptoms of alienation can be symptoms of many things beside alienation itself, and yet be labeled as alienation for convenience or other purposes. Generally speaking, situations fuel alienation rather than do particular individuals. When a young person feels her or his parents at war with each other, whether or not one or both parents are expressing any pressure to take sides, chances are that the child will experience such pressure. While most children heal from the effects of this tug of war, adults must be alert to the possibility of deep and long lasting consequences. Parents and other relatives must be particularly careful to avoid fueling any alienation and to realize that everyone around the child can play a role in preventing alienation.

TOLERANCE

Of course it is not only fighting parents who teach abuse and violence as a way of life, an acceptable medium of exchange. It is the media and the world around children as well. Yes, we live in a world where violence is virtually normal. Everywhere they look, and a large part of what they learn in school, tells children that violence works, that violence is part of life and part of history. The tolerance of violence is instilled so deeply in children, and yet so invisibly. Children's nervous systems react to violence, and record their reactions to violence. Repeated exposure to violence dulls some of the response to it, and generates a mental and biochemical system of incorporating this reality, perhaps a desensitization to it as the brain cells open more and more receptor sites that become hooked—hungry for the roller coaster ride the adults' (and the world's) patterns take them on.

Parents can counter this trend by visibly practicing positive conflict resolution processes and telling their children this is what they are doing. Rising above abuse and violence is possible and can become a way of life, first in the home. No, we cannot turn the hands of time back, but we can start now, and teach our children well—or at least better than we have done so far.

CHAPTER 12

The Child in the Physical Environment

> And then she took a long breath and looked behind her up the long walk to
> see if any one was coming. No one was coming. No one ever did come, it
> seemed, and she took another long breath, because she could not help it, and
> she held back the swinging curtain of ivy and pushed back the door which
> opened slowly—slowly.
>
> Then she slipped through it, and shut it behind her, and stood with her
> back against it, looking about her and breathing quite fast with excitement,
> and wonder, and delight.
>
> She was standing *inside* the secret garden.
>
> Frances Hodgson Burnett, *The Secret Garden*

The young person's physical surroundings have a profound although relatively unheralded influence on the development of her or his mental abilities. Whether the child is at home, at school, at preschool, or somewhere
else, the quality and characteristics of the environment are critical. Look at
the place or places where your child spends the most time. This is likely to
be home and school or preschool. As a parent, you have the greatest say in
the nature of the home environment. If you are a teacher, you have the classroom to design as an intelligence-promoting environment.

ORGANIZATION

Of all the physical characteristics of a child's environment, organization is
one of the most critical. This does not mean that children need an
extremely organized environment. It does mean that a certain level of organization is important and that a child feels the effects of this organization in

many ways. Note that each of these points applies to children and teens of all ages. I say child below meaning anyone eighteen and under. Note that much of this is relevant to adults as well:

- A child who knows where to find most of her or his shoes, shirts, and other regularly needed items most of the time feels secure about this and benefits from this security.
- A child who knows that there is a neat, organized area in the house where she or he can do homework each day can count on this and will be more likely to return to that spot again and again.
- A child studying in a relatively neat, organized spot tends to concentrate more, do neater work, and complete more work.
- When a child regularly experiences organization in her or his physical environment, that child's mind adapts to this reality in subtle ways. This is especially true as that child matures. She or he becomes increasingly involved in maintaining the organization of the living space, and of the mental space as well ("keeping the place neat").

When a child contributes to the organization of the physical space in which she or he lives and works, there are many positive effects. These include:

- Some sense of control over the immediate environment grows within the child. This increasing mastery of the physical environment spills over into an increasing sense of mastery over her or his emotional and conceptual (thinking) environments. The outer world can reflect the inner world and vice versa.
- The child's efforts to organize some of the objects in the physical outer world serve as valuable training for organizing thoughts in the inner world.
- An ongoing sense of accomplishment is generated. With that sense comes a feeling that all kinds of things can indeed be accomplished.

Organization and participating in creating organization can play a wonderful role in the realizing of mental potential. There is a security in organization, a security that relieves tension and allows the child the emotional space to develop. As a child once explained to me: "Chaos is exotic. It's strange 'cuz it's not usual. It makes little children trip and fall. It makes some big kids act wild." (I was surprised at her use of the word "exotic." It is an unusual word for a child, especially at six years old, which she was at the time.)

A note here. Like anything good, organizing can go too far. Ongoing extreme pressure to keep everything neat, in its place, and organized can grow into an ongoing emotional crisis state or even an obsession that may or may not be expressed by the child in a way the parents can see it. Be careful about this. There is a fine balance between a healthy level of organization and one that is not. Preoccupation with the order of things can become just that—a *preoccupation*. When organizing does become a *preoccupation*, it then comes *before* homework, sleeping, playing—living and learning.

FREEDOM

Freedom to explore the surrounding space provides essential stimulation to a child's mind. Be certain that the child's physical environment offers as much freedom as possible. First, take care of all safety issues in an age-appropriate way (for example, baby gates for crawling and toddling children, matches hidden from children until they are at least ten years old, alcohol out of reach, out of access, and out of sight of adolescents—better yet no alcohol on the premises). Once you have addressed safety issues, define spaces and areas in the home, yard, neighborhood, and even city (for your older children) that you permit the child to explore. Try to communicate that you are providing freedom rather than taking it away.

RESOURCES

Among the details that should be included in a child's environment are learning resources. Children who have begun to read and spell will need a dictionary and likely a computer as well. Older children should have access to dictionaries, encyclopedias, computers, and so on. The technologies available to adults in these times are something children and teens are exposed to. Learning to use these technologies in safe and productive ways must be part of the education young people receive.

Remember that non technological learning resources are also important. All children will benefit from color charts, templates for drawing shapes, art supplies, and other resources that do not require electricity. Keep these resources within the child's reach so that the child may use them without asking for help to do so. When a child can use resources on her or his own initiative, without an adult making it possible, a child can initiate a private, self-directed learning and creative experience.

GUIDANCE

Parents, teachers, and other involved adults serve as mentors and guides through the world, especially the physical world. What this means is that adults show children "how to be" in a museum, a library, a forest, on a cliff, in a toy store, and so on. Beginning at an early age, take the role of guide on your visit to "planet earth" with your child—"how to survive here" is of course on the parent's mind although not expressed in these words.

This parent or guide must consciously aim to become a follower at times. This is increasingly true as the child ages. The child should be encouraged to lead the adult as often as possible. For example, let your child take you on a tour of a forest or botanical garden. Let your child show you around her or his room. Let your child explain the way she or he sees something.

COLOR

Children are very sensitive to color. Very young children are actually more aware of contrasts between colors than of colors. I saw this first-hand. When my daughter was a baby, the room in our house that had served as my office became her nursery. I had decorated my office in black and white a few years before she was born, and bits of that color scheme survived my painting the walls a rich pink and the trim a bright sky blue. The result was a black and white and blue and pink room. I was astounded to find that the first parts of her room that held her visual attention were the black and white curtains and pillows. This was so much the case that I wore my black and white striped sweaters and shirts almost every day the first several months. It was not long that the colors were more attention-grabbing than the black and whites, and this attention to contrasts over colors themselves faded away.

Use color as an invitation to notice, to enjoy, and to explore the environment. As your own children mature, give them increasing say as to the colors they wear and see (in their bedrooms). Use your judgment and say "no" whenever you feel that you must. (I remember a little boy who at about five years of age wanted his room painted black.)

DETAIL BUT NOT CLUTTER

Detail is essential in a child's environment. However, let us not confuse clutter with detail. As I have said elsewhere, the physical environment should be organized and not chaotic. It should offer many attractive details of interest. Here is another topic that children and teens can learn the inner workings of—the difference between detail and clutter. Talk about it, have fun with the topic. Find words to explain this in words that work for you and your child. Know this: detail has a logic, an arrangement to it, while clutter does not. Clutter is largely counterproductive; detail can be the opposite. (I say this knowing that certain creative adults find that some degree of clutter brings out their creativity. Still, children of all ages are not necessarily ready to realize their highest learning potentials in cluttered environments. Again, a balance is always important.)

BASIC ELEMENTS OF PHYSICAL CARE

Especially during early childhood, the stage of life when physical growth is most accelerated, the quality of the physical environment is critical. It is in providing a sound physical environment that parents protect, nurture, and develop the bodies of their children. Remember, the body houses every organ, bone, and cell of the child. The body houses the brain and affects mental development.

Physical care is many things—nourishment, stimulation, and protection. Physical protection involves an awareness of basic health requirements, efforts to spot any problems, challenges and or ailments, and awareness of the degree of contagion associated with particular illnesses. The likelihood of contagion among large groups of unrelated children who spend long hours together in relatively small spaces (such as classrooms) increases in crowded settings. General upkeep, cleanliness, and sanitation are more difficult to sustain in overpopulated environments. Time-pressed caregivers may fail to separate infected children from the group and may overlook procedures such as thorough rather than quick hand washing. We see this in some crowded child-care settings, but know this can take place wherever caregivers (likely through no fault of their own) are time poor and stressed.

All physical development is dependent on nutritional intake. Parents and educators must not only understand dietary requirements of young children and the developmental processes that depend on nutrition, they must be certain children get enough but not too much to eat, and proper nutrition, not junk (empty calorie) food and candy. Note that calories alone do not determine proper nutrition.

Physical development is often regarded as something that is visibly apparent through changes in the form of either bodily or motor developments. However, beneath the surface, many internal developments are taking place. For one thing, massive changes in the brain and nervous system occur in childhood. Myelinization is a process in which particular nerve fibers are coated, or sheathed, in a fatty substance called myelin. During early infancy and early childhood, myelinization proceeds most rapidly. Significant myelinization is also believed to occur between the ages of six and ten, when the corpus callosum (connecting the nerve fibers of the brain's right and left hemispheres) is presumed completed, as are the parietal and frontal areas of the cortex, the outer layer of the brain. According to many sources, some myelinization continues in certain parts of the brain until at least the age of thirty, if not far longer.

Neurologists suggest that the myelinization process, which occurs only in the higher regions of the brain, affects learning, the development of language and memory, and the control of impulses. Analytic and spatial abilities may be connected where the hemispheres of specialized regions of the brain are linked by myelinized nerves. Where myelinization fails to occur, learning and physical disabilities may ensue. Other nervous system changes include the speeding up of the brain waves and the changing of sleep patterns during childhood. Fine motor and hormonal developments also occur during infancy. All of these less visible physical developments accompany the development of gross motor skills (including walking and running) during childhood. Physical activities can help promote neuromuscular and as well as actual mental development.

What is it about the physical environment that gives direct impetus to individual development? There are several examples of environmental characteristics that affect development. For example, experiments have suggested that the blink response (normally beginning early in infancy) develops an average of three weeks earlier in young infants who have been regularly provided with a stable visual pattern over their cribs to focus on (for at least one-half hour a day). There are also numerous reports of the negative effects of a troubled environment, or of a deprived, unstimulating environment, on development.

Never can there be enough concern directed at the safety of an environment in which a child is cared for. Toys, equipment, building designs, and nearby streets or parking lots all represent potential dangers to children. The physical environment must be regulated and constantly monitored for safety.

Parents who are evaluating the physical environments of their children's preschools and schools (as well as their own homes) will want to examine the following:

- the condition of the surrounding neighborhood, its safety, the level of noise, and the pollution
- the square footage of indoor and outdoor areas in terms of adequate space per child

- the condition of a cafeteria or kitchen, the toilets, the bathing facilities, the equipment, and the supplies
- the organization of the space the children use
- the safety of the grounds, accesses, and equipment
- the means of controlling indoor air quality, such as heating, cooling, and ventilation
- the aesthetics and comfort of the physical surroundings
- the extent to which physical surroundings provide an opportunity for privacy, a sense of order, and a stimulating experience
- the degree to which the physical environment invites learning, thinking, and concentration

EKISTICS

Space, time patterns, things, and people are real elements of the child's environment. A child's environment influences her or his activities. This is the work of "spatial forces," as they are called in the terminology of *ekistics*. All spatial forces are either directional or nondirectional. Directional forces attract or repel. For example, the front of a classroom, a family dinner table, a large tree, or a playground fence attracts or constrains the physical activity of adults and children in the vicinity. Nondirectional forces do not attract or repel, but have other sensory effects. These include the size of a room, the proportions of a building, and the textures of some upholstery. Each of these spatial forces affects behavior within their physical spaces. Study corner and special places for particular possessions are also important. From an ekistic perspective, the child's environment should if possible have special areas for which particular activities are consistently designated, such as a dining area, a sleeping area, a work table, and a place to dress.

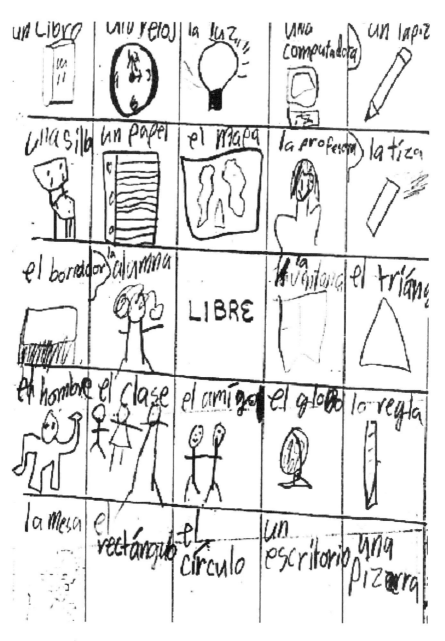

Developing Mental Abilities (Illustration by Evacheska deAngelis)

Part Four

Encouraging Mental Abilities

CHAPTER 13

Developing Children's Mental Abilities

"How is the plan coming, Charlotte? ..."

"Oh, it's coming all right," she said, lightly. "The plan is still in its early stages and hasn't completely shaped up yet, but I'm working on it."

"When do you work on it?" begged Wilbur.

"When I'm hanging head-down at the top of my web. That's when I do my thinking, because then all the blood is in my head."

E. B. White, *Charlotte's Web*

Children develop mental abilities under almost any circumstance. Yet, parents and teachers can make a significant difference in the degree to which children realize their mental potentials. How?

- By recognizing that you, as parent and or teacher, have a great influence on the development of your child's mind.
- By believing that you *can* help raise your child's mental ability.
- By letting your child know, from the start (even if you believe that your child is too young to understand), that you value mental ability.
- By helping your child develop an awareness of her or his own mental activity.
- By teaching your child that everyone can learn and that learning is an ongoing process.
- By taking an active role in your child's mental development.

In this chapter, I discuss some methods of taking an active role in the mental development of your child. These include teaching strategy selection, encouraging verbal ability, teaching spatial skills, developing number skills, using music in learning, emphasizing organizational skills, emphasizing the recognition of differences (in shapes, colors, words, etc.), learning relativity, heightening concentration, strengthening memory, and upping brain speed.

TEACH STRATEGY SELECTION

Communicate the importance of selecting a strategy for problem-solving or doing any task. Again, as discussed in the first few chapters of this book, we must ask children to consider the existence of a level of thinking *above* just thinking directly about the subject or issue at hand. The concept, even the word strategy, may sound too complex to ask a child to learn; however, you *can* teach a child to think about the concept of a problem-solving strategy, even from an early age. ("How do you solve problems, Marty? What are the steps you use?") In fact, if you begin mentioning strategy from the age of three, and slowly increasing the complexity of your comments about strategy, your child will become quite accustomed to the word and the concept and incorporate it into her or his own world view. Just talking about strategy paves the way for a greater understanding of it. And strategy is a thought process, a mental discipline.

We can teach strategy in short little clips in the early years. Consider this conversation I had with my six-year-old daughter. My notes about the conversation are in italics:

"If I ask you what seven take away two is, how do you get the answer?" *(I presented the problem to be solved.)*

"Well, I go: one plus one is two, and one plus one plus one is three, and one plus one plus one plus one is four, and one plus one plus one plus one plus one is five, then one more is six, and five plus one plus one is seven." *(She uses her fingers but is not looking at them.)*

"So, then, what is seven take away two?"

"Five."

"Right. How did you get that?" *(This "how" is asking about the strategy the child used.)*

"Because if six is after five and seven is after six, then if you take two away, the seven and the six, you get the five." *(Interesting method.)*

"Good. So what was your strategy?" *(Here is my chance to use the word strategy.)*

"What's strategy?" *(Great! She asked.)*

"Strategy is a plan for figuring something out, the way you figure something out."

"Once Julia's cat said, 'Mickey'." *(Her mind wanders.)*

"Oh, her cat can talk? I like the idea that a cat talks.... So strategy is how you figure something out." *(I come back to my point.)*

"Yeah."

"So what strategy did you use to get the answer to seven take away two?" *(I want more on the strategy.)*

"I used my head."

"I thought you counted on your fingers." *(I dig for more information.)*

"No I didn't, I went like this." *(She looked away from her hands while bending her fingers back one by one.)*

"O.K. So, what would you say that the strategy here is? Using your head—while using your fingers but not looking at them—while you think?" *(I say this slowly.)*

"Yeah. One plus one plus one."

"So do your fingers help?"

"No. My fingers do not help."

"So what do your fingers do when you do that?"

"It just ... it just feels good on my fingers."

"And do the fingers help you keep track of what you are thinking, even when you don't look at them?"

"No. No, they do not. They help me feel sure." *(So moving fingers is part of the strategy. They help her feel sure.)*

"Sure of what?"

"Sure of the numbers I am thinking about.... It's like the fingers are in my mind." *(She may be visualizing the problem and its solving as part of her strategy.)*

"O.K. Let's try another problem. What is seven take away three?" *(I introduce another problem as a way of extending strategy past the first example.)*

"Seven take away three is four." *(She answers quickly)*

"How did you do that?"

"I just did it. I didn't have to count, because I'm in first grade and you know more things in first grade than you do in kindergarten." *(Perhaps sheer memory is used here, with no obvious strategy. Of course finding answers in memory is a strategy. Or perhaps short term memory still held the picture of the fingers and they did the work here.)*

"And what about six take away three?" *(She thinks a little longer.)*

"Uh ... it's three. Let's see ... six take away three is three."

"Right. And how did you get that one?"

"Three plus three is six, so six take away three is three."

"Oh, so you added first and then subtracted." *(This is a strategy.)*

"Yes, I knew the adding part already but not the subtracting part."

"But on seven take away three you knew the answer right off."

"Yes, I've known it since I was a baby."

"I didn't know that, wow. You heard it somewhere. You remembered it."

"I said I knew it when I was a baby. I saw it on Sesame Street I think." *(Drawing on one's memory is a strategy.)*

"It sounds as if you used a different strategy for each problem I gave you today." *(I introduce the idea that there is more than one strategy for solving a particular type of problem.)*

"What's a strategy?" *(Good. We come back to strategy.)*

"Strategy is the way you solve a problem. Remembering is a strategy. You used memory and other strategies here as well. *(She was listening closely here, so I went on.)* You can *remember* the answer to seven take away three. You can *add* three plus three to get six, and then you can *figure out* what six take away three is. You can *count* in your head while using your fingers but not looking at them to get seven take away two. Remembering, adding, using your fingers, these are all strategies for figuring something out. *(I realized I was going on a little too long and decided to ask a question, to re-engage my listener so to speak.)* So what do you think strategy is?"

"I think it's when, um ... um, like what my friend's dad did with the hard puzzle." *(She gives an example.)*

"Ah. What did he do? Solve a hard puzzle?"

"Yes."

"Did he have a strategy?"

"Yes."

"What was his strategy?"

"He put the puzzle pieces behind the other ones with the same shape, sort of the same shape, that would go in the same place and if the first ones didn't work, he tried more and if the second ones didn't work, then tried the next ones." *(So she seems to understand that strategy is the method used to solve a problem—in this case trying puzzle pieces for fit in steps.)*

"So strategy is the way you think about something when you're trying to figure it out." *(I summarize.)*

"Yeah."

I stopped there and we went back to the matter of the talking cat. Keep your discussion of strategy to the point. If the child's mind wanders once or twice, bring it back. If it wanders five or more times, phase out the session and come back to the topic again later. Children will become increasingly conscious of their use of mental strategies if you talk to them about this.

You do not have to teach all there is to know about strategy in one sitting. In fact, do not try. Over the years, your conversations will become increasingly sophisticated. In the mean time, the value of strategy in thinking things through will be instilled.

ENCOURAGE VERBAL ABILITIES

Encourage the child to participate in discussions. Talk to her or him about ideas, about how things work, about what things mean, about anything you can talk about in a low pressure, friendly situation. Remember that a discussion is not a monologue. A child learns by listening but also by engaging, even teaching, by explaining functions (how and why things work), giving definitions (what words mean and how they are used), and describing processes (what leads to what and under what circumstances). Remember that no explanation that requires thinking and creativity is ever entirely wrong. Get your child used to putting thoughts into words. Make it clear that discussions are ways of moving toward new ideas, new way of seeing things or more about the same things, new understandings. Value every step along the way, and make it clear that you do. The process of thinking something through and talking about it as you do is as important as the outcome of this process.

Give your child words to put thoughts into and words that will stimulate thinking. Introduce new words such as strategy, complex, abstract, fragile, absurd, chaotic, and any other words that come to your mind. Keep a notebook to help you remember what words and concepts you are introducing. Don't make this a high pressure "you must learn this now" activity. Understand that it may take years for a child to really master the use of a complex word. You have time. Begin as young as you can, and remember, if you didn't start early, it is never too late to begin. Expand you child's vocabulary potential simply by using certain words again and again. Begin when the child is very young—when she or he still says "ga-ga da-da." Say lists of polysyllabic words in sets which share a similar sound, such as "fabulous, hazardous, wondrous, tremendous, stupendous." As the child ages, help the child slowly repeat these words. Stimulate memory, word recognition, and clear thought.

ENCOURAGE EXPLANATIONS OF HOW THE WORLD WORKS

Listen carefully. If the child's explanations are not entirely correct, help this child reformulate them, but do this gently. I discuss the process of reformulation itself in depth later in this book. Here, let's focus on the general character of the process. Ease the child into a revision of her or his understanding of the particular function, definition, or process you think is incorrect. Do not demand that the child just change her or his mind. Do not criticize or reprimand a child for her or his incorrect information. Do not, for example, say, "No a car does not run on air and that's that," or "No, you're wrong, 'constant' is not a flying star, that's a comet," or "No, the sun does not turn off when it goes down, it moves and is seen from another part of the Earth." Flat, blunt, abrupt corrections, unless delivered with the utmost care, can have negative effects. Children can feel frowned upon, embarrassed, ashamed, and or rebellious in response. Instead, engage the child in discussion. It might go as follows.

"Oh, I see. You believe that the sun turns off at night. That's a good idea. It's one way to explain what the sun does. Other people have other ways of explaining this. Some say that the sun does not turn off, but that it just goes and shines somewhere else, that it makes daylight on the other side of the Earth. Let's talk about this difference in these ways of explaining what the sun does at night."

Take your child's ideas seriously. Allow for the existence of more than one explanation or definition. Talk about each explanation as well as about the one that you consider more correct or more reasonable. Ask your child to summarize the conversation. You might say one of these things:

"Okay. Let's summarize."

"Whatever were we talking about . . . what was the subject?"

"What kind of conversation (scientific, emotional) did we have about that subject?"

"What was the course of the conversation? What happened first, second (and so on)?"

Framing conversations and thoughts is yet another way to teach the child to think about thinking. This also helps build writing skills, because writing requires defining or framing a topic and also thinking through steps in discussing or explaining the topic.

TEACH SPATIAL ABILITIES

Spatial ability develops with experience in space, in the space around us we call our environment. It is the ability to relate areas, objects, and their shapes and sizes to each other. Although much of the learning in this area is learning by doing, there is also a lot to be said for learning by thinking. A child is never too young to hear you ask, "Do you think that will fit there?" This question triggers wondering, contemplation. The child's mind *sees* the problem in reality (the yarn that will or will not fit through the eye of the needle, the puzzle piece that will or will not fit next to another piece, the desk that will or will not fit under the window). The child's mind also sees, visualizes—builds a mental construction of—the problem in her or his mind. Babies and toddlers build the ability to visualize, to think about spatial questions by physically handling objects and attempting to make them fit. Older children are pressed to develop more powerful mental abilities when they are asked to visualize first. Begin asking a three-year-old to think before trying to make something fit. Do not push children this age to visualize a spatial problem. Six-year-olds are often quite ready to consciously attempt spatial problems in their minds. By the age of nine or ten, children should be encouraged to regularly practice visualizing to answer even complex spatial questions.

DEVELOP NUMBER SKILLS

Life is full of opportunities for mathematical analysis. Take advantage of opportunities to do mathematical analysis with your child. Regardless of the child's age, you can regularly involve your child in counting, measuring, adding, estimating, and other procedures. The older the child is, the more mathematical analysis she or he can do independently of you. Ask older children to double check restaurant bills, calculate the miles per gallon of gas your car is getting, balance your checkbook, calculate the down payment on your house, and so on. If your child is too young to do such things, let your child watch you and, as the child matures, explain what you are doing again and again. Eventually, have the child participate, first in small ways, then in big ways. Under the right circumstances, many number skills can be more readily learned in daily life than in the classroom.

USE MUSIC IN LEARNING

Music is the key to the heart, the soul, the mind, and the body. Bring music into your child's life from birth or, if you are adventurous, from before birth by putting head phones on the mother's belly. Even prenatal and newborn infants can feel rhythms. A rhythm is a repeated sound pattern, a repeating beat. Feeling and hearing rhythm from a young age helps the child's mind learn to recognize patterns. Because pattern recognition is an essential skill in reading, mathematical reasoning, and abstract thinking, children can benefit by being stimulated with rhythmic music.

Children also gain verbal skills by learning songs. Play the same songs again and again for very young children. They begin learning, remembering the tunes and the phonetic sounds that accompany the tunes long before they learn to talk. In memorizing even bits and pieces of songs, the mind of a baby opens storage compartments for future words. More vocabulary can thus be accumulated earlier in life.

Preschool and K-12 children can actually can learn to speak and spell more rapidly when music is applied. For example, you can teach your child to spell her or his whole name by picking an easy jingle or song and putting the spelling of the name to it. Sing this again and again with your child and eventually your child will sing it alone, and use this to spell her or his name earlier than one might expect. Selecting a tune is important. You must pick a tune you will not forget, maybe even for a year or two. You do not want to change the tune on the child as you go along. This is because the child learns the tune and connects the tune with the words.

EMPHASIZE ORGANIZATIONAL SKILLS

Teach the child to think clearly, and in an organized manner. "Easier said than done," I hear replied when I give this advice. This reply makes sense. After all, how does a parent or a teacher get into a child's mind and organize it?

However, there are ways in. By having your child do organizing exercises in the physical world, you are teaching the child's mind to organize objects. Organizing objects by size, color, purpose, age, value, or other categorical divisions demands that the mind organize ideas and concepts. Take advantage of the real and invented needs for organization. Have your child sort knives, forks, and spoons into separate containers. For young ones who should not handle dangerous utensils, cut up large chips of colored paper. Have them organize chips by color and, as they progress, by particular shades of particular colors. Children who cannot yet, without your help, sort whatever you give them to organize, should be assisted, never criticized, always applauded, in the organizing work you give them.

RECOGNIZE DIFFERENCES

Learning to identify large and small differences between things is part of learning to think. The organization activities referred to in the above section involve *differentiation*. Unless one can tell the difference between things being sorted, they will all fall into the same category. Look for opportunities to distinguish between types of dogs, flowers, books, foods, and so on. Look also for opportunities to observe finer differences among flowers on the same bush or among petals on the same flower.

LEARN RELATIVITY

Be sensitive to differences between differences. "That shoe and this shoe are a bit different from each other, but that shoe and that very tiny shoe are even more different from each other." When you are on the freeway, talk to your child about how cars are moving at different speeds. Look for cars that are moving at a very different speed from each other. Compare these differences to those between cars going close to the same speed. Talk about the differences between difference as much as possible. This teaches *relative differences*. It creates a slot in the mind for advanced comparison and highly abstract thinking.

HEIGHTEN CONCENTRATION, ALERTNESS, AND ATTENTION SPAN

Find ways to provide your child with concentration training. What do I mean by concentration training? People who become highly proficient at something that requires a lot of practice, such as playing the violin, playing chess, or performing ballet, have had to learn to concentrate to develop their special skills. Once concentration is developed, the ability to concentrate can be transferred from one subject to another. This ability to concentrate is especially potent if an individual begins developing it at an early age and continues developing it through adolescence and during adulthood.

Sometimes we forget that learning to focus, to concentrate, is the primary goal. Our children may specialize—develop expertise—in something very early and stay with it for many years (as we see young Olympic gymnasts do), or they may delve into something for a while and then move on. Parents too often chastise children for "not staying with anything long enough" and should be careful about this criticism. If parents feel themselves applying intense pressure and or anger or bribery to get their children to stick to things, a step back should be taken right away. What is the real goal of all this? This is not to say that giving up on an activity, or on several activities in a row, is to be favored. However, exploration and experience are valuable, quite often at least as valuable as the outcome of (violin, piano, drum) lessons themselves.

All this being said, it is still true that parents do well to encourage (again, not force, not demand, but definitely provide a structure for) their children to learn to be an expert at something. The exercise of learning to become an expert, or even trying to learn to become an expert, is what is most important. Too often we forget this. Even the exercise of learning to become an expert requires mental concentration and commitment over time, whether this time be hours or days or weeks or months or years. This type of experience gives a child important knowledge about her or his capacity to concentrate and to gain mastery via concentration. Experiences learning to concentrate can be built upon over time. Each experience of learning to concentrate and continuing to learn to concentrate on something in particular allows a child to learn (1) repeated, sustained, and cumulative goal-oriented concentration over a period of time; (2) confidence in her or his ever-growing ability to focus; and (3) variable concentration skills that can be transferred to other activities undertaken in childhood, adolescence, and adulthood.

Giving (remember giving is not forcing which is why I say giving) a child the experience of long-term concentration aimed at skill development in a single area or a few select areas also allows the child, and later the adult, to feel confident enough to undertake difficult things. All too often we don't attempt challenging things because we have never been led to believe that we can accomplish them. We do not believe in our own mental abilities because we have not experienced them. (Our parents cannot just expect us to do something well because they tell us to. They better allow us to experience increasing expertise by time trying, time doing, time focusing.)

Another approach to the development of concentration skills is direct training in concentration itself. Again, childhood is the best time to begin learning to concentrate deeply, but it is never too late. You can teach even an old dog some exciting new tricks. A few, very few, elementary, secondary, and high schools and colleges are now offering direct training in thinking skills. One of the many thinking skills that can be taught, or at least enhanced in the classroom, is concentration itself.

One of the essential elements of concentration education is understanding the essence of concentration. Ask yourself what you think the definition of concentration is. Then check your mind out—do it now—how closely are you concentrating on what you are reading here? How do you know? What can you do to focus in on this activity, this reading, right now? (By the way, reader, what did you think of just now when you read the word "focus," and what are you thinking of now that I ask this?)

You will learn a great deal about your child's mind by studying your own mind. Survey your knowledge of your own concentration activity:

- Have you ever been aware that you were concentrating intensely on something?
- Exactly how did you come to realize this?
- On what were you concentrating so intensely?
- On what types of activities do you concentrate intensely?
- Do you allow yourself to be distracted when you really do not want to concentrate?
- Are there particular times of day and places in which you concentrate best?

You can improve the workings of your mind and your child's mind by learning to concentrate. Your attention span will lengthen. You ability to work with complex ideas will grow. Your confidence will expand. You will know enough about what concentration is to share it with your child. Concentration skills are immensely valuable in developing intelligence.

STRENGTHEN MEMORY

Memory skills are also valuable. Memory plays a critical role in learning. Without memory, what can be learned can be lost. Furthermore, without remembering the simple facts, lessons, and concepts on which the next level of mental development is built, a child would not increase in mental ability. There are many scientific explanations for memory and learning. We can generalize or simplify them here this way: Bits of information are taken into the mind and held in the short-term memory. This information is identified, examined, applied, and its use repeated until it is permanent enough to be moved further in, embedded deeply in, the realm of permanent or long-term memory.

Memory can be strengthened with practice. Try to build these practice methods into your ongoing interactions with your child:

- memorizing sayings and poems
- remembering a series of events in detail
- remembering where things have last been seen
- remembering a whole story or a speech

UP BRAIN SPEED

Brain speed is the speed at which electrical impulses or signals move across the brain from one point to another. A brain can be and should be exercised. Just as you can help your child strengthen her or his memory, you can cultivate her or his brain speed. Runners who sprint in competition practice to increase speed. Thinkers—anyone using her or his brains—everyone that is—can practice to increase brain speed. Try activities such as these:

- Find a game or an object that has a light that blinks suddenly. Even a flashlight with a blinker button will do. The child should be required to do something immediately on seeing the light go on. If you are playing a manufactured game, such a requirement may be built in. Otherwise, create opportunities for your child to practice responding as rapidly as possible to a stimulus such as a light that suddenly and unpredictably blinks. The required response should be an easy one, involving a small motion of the hand or tap of the finger. Do this type of practice regularly and begin at as young an age as you can get your child to participate. Children and adults of all ages benefit from such practice, so do not avoid it if you have not started them young.
- Play games that encourage quick thinking. Aim the questions, the demands of the game, at the ability of the child. (Do not ask a one-year-old to spell "establishment" as rapidly as possible.) Try to select questions your child can answer. The goal here is getting known answers rapidly, not measuring whether or not the child can get them right. For example, let's say your child knows basic addition, but has learned it recently and is not very fast with the answers. Practice:

"What is two plus two?"

"Uh ... four."

"Good. One plus one?"

"Um ... uh ... um ... two."

"Now two plus two again."

"Four."

Continue this way whenever you find a chance. I am actually talking about a state of mind here: once you begin looking for opportunities to raise your child's mental abilities, you will find them everywhere. Have fun with this process.

CHAPTER 14

Teaching Creativity

We could do nothing without the help of my sister. You have no idea how wise she is. She has eyes, too! Why, she can see you, at this moment, just as distinctly as if you were not invisible; and I'll venture to say, she will be the first to discover the Gorgons.

Nathaniel Hawthorne, "A Gorgon's Head"

Intelligence finds its way into expression largely through what we can best describe as a sort of creativity. We often overlook the role of creativity in the expression of mental activity. Instead, we see only the most obvious signs of adult creativity, the most innovative inventions, the newest science fiction films, the most famous pieces of art. We notice children's wildest stories, brightest paintings, and loudest projections of their creativities.

Yet creativity is manifested in most every expression of the mind. Just turning an idea into an expression of that idea requires creative energy. Thinking about taking a drink of juice and then lifting the glass to one's lips and sipping the juice requires an ingenious transformation of thought into action. However, this and most simple actions like it are so common and so automatic that we rarely appreciate that transformation. Still, the things we do, the efforts we make, the thoughts we think, are the body of creativity. Life is a creative process.

THE CREATIVITY-ENHANCING ENVIRONMENT

When we seek to encourage creativity in children, we must begin with the assumptions that:

- life is a creative process;
- even the most simple, common acts are creative; and
- all transformation of ideas into efforts or actions is creative.

This means that the child in which you wish to encourage creativity *is already a creative being*. You are merely providing an environment that recognizes, expresses and enhances that creativity. Of course, adults can do much to create creativity-enhancing environments for children:

- First and foremost, adults must model creativity by painting, dancing, storytelling, and anything else that feels and is creative.
- Second, adults must make it clear that the positive use of creativity is appreciated, valued. Notice and approve children's creativity. Acknowledge adults' creativity as well. Be a frequent and willing audience for the expression of creativity through the arts and sciences. Everyone's taste patterns are different. Pick and choose from among a broad range of exhibitions, concerts, plays, shows; teach children to be good audience members and to appreciate creativity as the adults around them do.
- Third, make a conscious effort to introduce into children's lives activities that are aimed specifically at developing their own innate creativities (such as storytelling, playing charades, inventing little things).

SEEING RELATIONSHIPS AND CONNECTIONS

Once information has been stored in memory by the brain, it must be retrieved to be used. Retrieval usually involves some form of connection or association between whatever task the individual is performing and the stored (previously memorized) information. For example, if I ask a first- or second-grade child to tell me what eighty-six plus one is, that child may be reminded of other (blank) plus one type of questions. Knowing that one more than ten is eleven and one more than twelve is thirteen is helpful. Knowing that six plus one is seven is still more helpful.

The memory, six plus one is seven, is triggered by the sound of eighty-*six plus one*. The memory of adding one to any number is triggered by the sound of *plus one*. The mind connects the task at hand to previously stored information.

When a more complex task is presented, such as, "Think of a living thing that has fins but is not a fish," the mind must recall quite a bit of information. (1) A living thing is an animal or a plant. (2) A fin is a flat, arm-like part of some animal's body. (3) Plants do not have fins. (4) Fish have fins. (5) Seals and whales also have fins. (6) A seal is not a fish. (7) A whale is not a fish. Now the mind is retrieving several bits of information, each of which it may have learned and stored in memory at different times, under different circumstances, for different reasons. The child might have learned the term "living things" in preschool. She or he might have learned about fins on a family trip to the zoo. Other information may have come in at other times. The child must relate the question being asked to information taken in at other times and then put it all together.

The more that a piece of information is connected, interconnected, to other information, the greater the chance it will be retrieved, remembered. We can help children become conscious of the importance of connecting information by talking to them about how bits of information can be connected to each other. Just talking about connecting thoughts helps a child become more aware of the possibilities of doing so. Make this a recurring conversation over time, over years if you can.

DEVELOPING ASSOCIATION SKILLS

The ability to connect or *associate* information is applied so frequently, and is so ever-present, that we rarely think about it. However, this ability, and many of the mental skills it depends on, can be taught and even enhanced. When a child is encouraged to connect ideas, that child's creativity is being encouraged. The connection of what may be, for the child, otherwise unconnected ideas, concepts, or images, is a creative act. It requires the creation of a link between bits of information.

Teach your child about the linking process:

- Talk about it quite often.
- Point out links that can be made.
- Aim your examples of association or linking at the child's mental level.
- Play association games such as, "I'm thinking of something big and red that starts with an 'a.'" Although you may be thinking of an apple, do not hold the child to a particular answer. The goal is to associate and to be creative, not to be right.
- Play sentence and story completion games.
- Play charades.

INTERDISCIPLINARY ADVENTURES

Children of all ages benefit tremendously when they see how different pieces of information, various subjects, and seemingly separate abilities can be related to each other. Use art and music to teach verbal skills in the child's first and then second (or foreign) language. Employ the use of art supplies when teaching children scientific, mechanical, and biological things. When studying history, consider the dress, the music, the food, the art, the family life, and the culture as well as wars and governments of the time being studied. Give children a deep appreciation for the relationship between disciplines by relating the disciplines for the child until she or he takes over. For example, show how geometry is both math and art. If you know music, show how music and math are related by counting out beats per measure and treating each note as a fraction of a pie. Connecting fields of study can spur great intellectual creativity in people of all ages.

FUEL INQUIRY

Did you, as a child, ask what seemed, to adults, to be too many questions? Encourage this asking in children. Inquiry is creative and essential to mental development. When I say this, I hear parents reply that they want to respond to their children's incessant questioning, but that it is just too much and too intrusive and too out of control. What I suggest is that busy parents set an official and regular question-answering time. The children asking the questions (and if they are too young, their parents and siblings) can write down or draw the questions in order to remember them. If children have saved no questions for the scheduled question-answering session, encourage them to make them up on the spot. Set an example of this inquiry process by making up your own questions. Teach question asking, inquiry, to all children of all ages, regardless of their original levels of question-asking. Even if a child is not a question-asker, she or he will be inspired by these question-asking sessions or games.

TEACH CHILDREN TO CHOOSE CREATIVE APPROACHES

Always seek the creative way. Solving math problems or brain twisters together with a child is a wonderful way to teach creativity. Emphasize the fact that there is always more than one way to get the answer. Courses in creativity frequently place greater emphasis on the number of ways of solving a particular math (or other) problem than on the right answer to that problem. And this is good. Exploration of processes and paths to solving a problem is at least as, if not more, important than solving the problem—a least while a child.

ENCOURAGE FREEDOM OF THOUGHT

Raise independent thinkers. Freedom is one of the greatest and yet most elusive qualities of life that we can pass on to our children. Children can learn, must learn, that there is more than one way to solve a problem, to see the world, to feel, and to think. Make this a topic of conversation throughout childhood (including adolescence). Parents sometimes shy away from this endeavor because they fear it encourages rebellion. It may do so, to some extent, but the level of rebellion a particular child expresses will not be increased significantly by this ongoing conversation. Questioning authority is an essential skill in a functional democracy. So is respect for authority. Let your child hear and see *you* doubt particular ideas, laws, and politicians. Let your child understand that while you exercise your right to think independently, you respect the process and structure of society.

CHAPTER 15

Learning to Learn

As a child (between four and seven years old), I saw in the outside world only those objects which were useful to my pleasure. These were above all, rocks, trees, and rarely more than one object at once. I remember that for at least two summers I saw nothing of my surroundings but one large rock which was located about 800 meters from the village, that rock and objects relating directly to it.

Alberto Giacometti, "Yesterday, Moving Sands"

Learning is a creative process. It is also a selective process: The mind, in its natural creativity, selects information to be operated on and stored. We can call this process of creative selection, operation and storage "learning." Children's minds can be trained to become more attentive to this remarkable process of selection, operation and storage—of learning. Children's minds can *learn to learn*.

In this chapter, I discuss some important aspects of learning and of learning to learn. Read this chapter when you have time and some quiet in which to think. Parts of this chapter may require some real concentration. If you read these parts again a few times and think carefully about what is being said, it all will come to you, either while you are reading or some time later. Apply as much of what you read as you can to your own understanding of your own thought processes. The more adults know about the processes of thinking and learning, the more they can make children aware of the processes.

Let's begin with the very basic process of learning to see, of becoming aware of seeing, of taking in visual information. This will help us understand the way children's minds work when they are learning. It will also help us teach children about how their minds work. The more children know about how their minds work, the more they can make their own minds work well. (Note that we choose to use seeing as the example here, however, we could also use other sensory functions such as hearing, and even feeling via the sense of touch, which function in terms of selecting what is sensed by the mind and perceived by the person.)

THE AUTOMATIC LEARNING OF ILLUSION

So much of the learning we do is done automatically. If we seek to enhance the learning process, we have to be able to take portions of the process off automatic. Understanding what it means to take the process off of automatic is the first step.

We can gain an understanding of what we do automatically, without thinking about it, by considering the process of seeing. Most of the seeing that we do is automatic. Somehow, quite subconsciously, we do learn to see. We also learn to have our minds change the things that we see. Consider the process of "form completion." Form completion is something the mind does—an illusion the mind creates. In form completion, the mind provides a whole picture of an otherwise discontinuous or incomplete subject. For example, a picture of a broken circle may be seen as a picture of a whole, unbroken circle. During this form completion, information about circles is drawn from one's memory, from stored recollections of previous experiences with circles. This information about the true nature of circles is added to the inadequate data regarding the present experience of a broken circle. Clinical tests show that people who are shown, in rapid succession, pictures of incomplete circles and other basic forms complete them at high speeds. In fact, they do not know that they are completing them. They instead report that they see the incomplete figures as complete or whole figures. The broken forms are mentally completed, automatically *fixed*, by a process I like to call *not-seeing*, the not-seeing of the gaps in the incomplete figures.

We all do a great deal of not-seeing. A very common, but more complicated version of automatic form completion is taking place every time we see our entire field of vision without gaps, despite our retinal blind spots and scars. Our eye movements compensate for our blind spots. They allow all points within the visual field to be "seen" by the retina. A whole picture is compiled through this automatic scanning process. We do this type of form completion in order to see. We do this not-seeing in order to see, or convince ourselves that we see.

Our automatic completion of otherwise partial pictures and fragmented information has true survival value. We learn to do this quite naturally. No one teaches us. It is instinct. What this means is that the world we see is an illusion, one which we construct through automatic processes such as form completion. We construct whole images of our otherwise fragmented pictures of our environments. Although these whole pictures are basically illusions, they are our everyday realities. We must always remember that a child, just as an adult, constructs a personal reality and then lives in it.

Another form of ongoing illusion, not-seeing, is the perception of color. The "seeing" of color is a mental translation of incoming data regarding variations in wavelengths of light. This translation is subjective; it is part of the process of creating, inventing, a picture of reality. Every perception of color is an illusion. We do not see colors as they really are. Two different shades or colors can appear to be the same, two identical colors can look entirely different. An orange may look one way next to a bright red object, and much brighter next to a black object.

And so, one of the parts of reality that we and our children take very much for granted—the existence of color—is quite illusory. The differences in colors that we see are just our mental interpretations of what is really out there.

It is important that we share this understanding about the mind's role in creating reality with our children, even the young ones. Our minds are so powerful that they tell us what we see in the world around us—even if we do not see it all or see it accurately or see it consistently. Talk about these concepts with children. Show them books with optical illusions in them. Get color chips from paint stores. Cut up these color chips and let children see how the same color looks different when the color next to it changes.

AWARENESS OF CHANGE AND DIFFERENCE

The illusions of form completion and color are part of a larger process of automatically "learning" about one's environment. Most of what we and our children see and know, we see and know because we can tell the difference between it and what is next to it. Our ability to recognize changes and differences in the terrain of our realities is essential in learning. It *is* learning.

Let us return to the process of seeing. Vision problems teach us a lot about the seeing process. Cataract patients consistently report an immediate awareness of a change following an operation to remove their cataracts. Once the cataract is removed, the newly regained visual field takes on character; it begins to reveal variations in light, color, and detail. Specific colors can be named within days of the operation. Many patients progress further, quickly identifying forms and patterns they are beginning to see again, based on the visual memories they accumulated before they developed cataracts.

On the other hand, a person who has been blind since birth, and who eventually has a surgical correction of this condition, does not see as readily as many cataract patients when the problem is alleviated. In such instances, this blind individual has no sight to be regained; for these people, seeing with the eyes is a new experience. The cataract patients learned to see earlier in life and thus begin seeing after surgery more rapidly than the blind patients who have never seen before. Vision is a learned process, and it takes time to learn to see. New learning, new detection of similarities and differences, is rapid if there is a good foundation or springboard of previous learning. Hint: To extend this discussion to general mental ability, let us say that whatever training we can give a child in seeing differences will be a springboard for later intellectual development. (Note that we must be careful here to make clear that this seeing of differences in the environment in no way refers to, or encourages, building social prejudices when seeing differences among people. What we are talking about here is the mind's ability to perceive, take in, store, remember, operate upon—and then build upon, bits of information from its environment.)

Seeing is a moldable process. Whether it is seeing or hearing or smelling or touching or tasting, the process of taking in information from the environment can be trained. Because seeing and other forms of sensing can be learned, these processes can also be refined, learned more precisely, with the right training. This is a valuable concept for parents and teachers. It takes learning to a more profound level. Both in school and at home, children take in information through their eyes and ears (and other senses). We can teach children how to take this information in more efficiently. We can teach children to better select and store information—to better learn. The way to teach this is to encourage a sensitivity to detail. Play games, hunt for differences and details in meadows, among flowers in the same bush, in faces, in everything you see with your child.

This is where understanding the importance of differences and similarities becomes a critical element in a child's mental development. For example, the more degrees of difference between light and dark that can be detected by a child, the more information the child draws from the environment. This sensitivity to differences is basic in sensory perception. Learning to see involves learning to see differences. After all, if no differences at all were perceived by the child, there would be no characteristics of reality detected; no information would be drawn from the environment. The child, seeing no differences, would be unable to function, unable to learn. As a child's awareness of differences increases, that child's perceptual precision increases: the child's learning ability increases as well.

We can help a child increase her or his perceptual precision (see, hear, and perceive more accurately). We must get right into the process of creating reality, of mapping the environment, with our children. The child (and any living organism) maps its environment based on the differences it perceives.

Learning to see (or hear or feel or taste or smell) is dependent on learning to appropriately map and categorize what is seen (or heard or felt or tasted or smelled) based upon differences. This mapping process is basic to learning in childhood. It *is* learning. Every child can recognize (and select) distinguishing characteristics. This permits her or him to classify objects and also ideas as once objects can be classified, the ability to classify abstract concepts—ideas—is gained.

As a child develops, she or he comes to better know the world by seeing finer distinctions among phenomena, improving her or his ability to differentiate by acquiring greater sensitivity to difference. For example, at one stage of development, a child looking out a window may or may not know whether she or he sees a succession of unfamiliar men or the same man going by again and again. The child does not necessarily distinguish between the two realities.

Learning to perceive involves learning to distinguish. Something is not seen (and not mapped, not categorized, not named) until it is differentiated from everything else. The growing child continuously refines his ability to perceive differences, to really see. This development does not cease in adulthood. We can and do continuously refine our seeing potentials, and with them, our mental potentials. Yet, no matter how many years of seeing we do, unless we can learn to "see" or differentiate something, to note what specific elements help to define it, it will remain virtually unseen, or mislabeled—generalized—as something else. For example, look at a field. If you do not know what is growing there, it remains a field. Once you learn to identify what grows there, its many living things, this field is no longer just a field, it is now a place where so many different things that you can name grow. We can make an effort to know what we are seeing—in fields, crowds of people, our environments. We can also expand this learning to "see" to hearing, touching, tasting. The more that we, as adults, work to refine our abilities to see, hear, taste, and smell, the more information we will take in from our environments—the more we will learn—because this is learning. The more we know what this process is about, the more we can share it with our children.

Now, let's take this discussion to the next level. I have been using the word seeing in a very literal way—talking specifically about the process of seeing with the eyes and relating it to other sensory processes. But we can also think of seeing as the seeing of ideas. The child learns to see ideas by recognizing them. Differences among concepts are recognized, in much the same way the child learns to pick out objects from the environment, to see objects as distinct from each other, as different and as identifiable as unique and separate. (The field is no longer just an actual field full of flowers, but a field full of ideas.) The child sees the order of ideas, fills in gaps in their forms, and seeks differences among them, organizes them, just as that child does with visual information coming in through the eyes. Children learn to "see" ideas and to organize them in their minds in terms of the similarities and differences (forming categories and orders of importance of ideas). The more children are aware that they are doing this, the greater their mental power.

LEARN TO LEARN

Children can thus consciously learn to learn. And then can consciously *learn to learn to learn*. It's all about becoming aware of various levels of thought and of thinking about thinking. Thinking and learning are so very linked—they are virtually one in the same once we accept the reality that every time we think we learn something, even if we learn that there is nothing to learn, because this is learning too.

So, let's talk about learning for a moment. Learning is change: First something is not known or its application (use) is not known, and then that something, once it is learned, is known. When a child changes her or his response to a signal or a stimulus, that child has learned. How many times do you have to say, "Do not touch that, it is hot and will burn you," before the child learns that it is hot and that is will burn—before the child learns this for her or him self? A change in response or reaction or recognition takes place each time something is learned by the mind.

The basis of all learning is the mere receipt of a signal. A buzzer rings, you hear it, that is all. The child touches the iron, does not react to the temperature of the iron—because maybe it is not on, not hot—that is all. This is zero level learning, or nonlearning. Why? It merely involves the receiving of a signal. Nothing is done with that signal except to receive it. There is no change in response to receiving the stimulus.

The next level of learning, or learning-one, simple single-loop learning, involves remembering information and one's reaction to the information. For example, when the child touches the now hot iron, that child's reflex is to remove her or his finger away from the hot metal. When presented with the hot iron again, the child may know better than to touch it. If the child does not touch the iron this next time, she or he has learned from previous experience. In this instance, the first level of learning has occurred.

A higher level of learning is learning-two, secondary learning. Having learned not to touch a hot iron, the child may be able to transfer the information about this experience to a new setting in which that child encounters a hot stove. If that child can take this knowledge and generalize it, that child will know not to touch any piece of hot metal or any hot utility. This child has now learned to learn. The child has used, has transferred, the learning about the hot iron to learn about other hot things.

Children (and adults) can learn to seek opportunities to learn information that they can apply again and again in different circumstances. In this manner, a child can become increasingly sensitive to the value of the things that she or he learns. That child can learn to spot transferability. You can help the child in this process. Having learned to learn once, the child can seek out other simple learning experiences that can lead to other second-level learning experiences. When a child does this, that child has learned not only how to learn, but how to learn to learn—that child can now learn to learn at will.

TEACH TRANSFERABILITY AWARENESS

Promote your child's development of this learning to learn at will:

- Begin talking about learning to learn as early as you can in the child's life. If you do not, or did not, begin in the second or third year of that child's life, then begin now. (Even the teenage years are not too late. In fact, adulthood is not too late.)

- Young children may not entirely understand what you are saying, but just keep mentioning learning to learn and finding examples of this in daily (or weekly) life. Just hearing you repeatedly identify and define the process causes the child's developing mind to create a space for incoming information about the process. Remember that ideas that are identified and named have a better chance of being remembered. You can help a child identify the specific mental process of learning to learn.

You open the door to second-level learning when you create opportunities for information transfer. As you create these opportunities, discuss the fact that you are creating them with your child. You can:

- Ask, if a cat is an animal and a dog is an animal, then what is a horse? Explain that knowing that cats, dogs, and horses have something in common and knowing that cats and dogs are animals may make it possible to move, spread, or transfer the knowledge to horses.

- Bring a child into discussions of sequence, such as yesterday was Saturday, so today is Sunday. Tomorrow is Wednesday, so today is Tuesday. Explain that knowing the order of all the days of the week helps one figure out which day comes before or after the other. We all transfer information about the order of days of the week all the time without realizing it. Having learned to transfer this knowledge of sequencing, we apply the ability to sequence in other areas, such as counting, alphabetizing, and so on. (If this sounds complicated, pat yourself on the back, as you've been doing this all your life.)

- Use (but do not seek) painful experiences, such as getting burned, as the chance to promote transfer. The hot iron burns, so what might the hot stove do? What is the lesson here? After the child answers this first question requiring the transfer of learning, you can help the child see how information about the hot iron can be applied or transferred to other hot things. "Anything hot can burn." (This sort of discussion can and should be done in a noncritical and nonpunishing voice.)

Infuse your children's thinking with an awareness of the second-level learning or transfer process. Climb into the child's thinking process. Be there with the child when the sparks fly from one part of the brain to another part of the brain. Look and listen for the little and big "aha's" that accompany second-level learning. Children miss many of their own "aha's." Help children identify these. Point out the occurrence or possible occurrence of transfer whenever you think that it has occurred. Explain what you see and think. Your explanations can become increasingly sophisticated over the years. You will be amazed at how quickly your child will catch up with you and then lead the way. Learning to learn depends on a combination of experience, knowledge, awareness, retention, recall, and a positive attitude about the process. It's easy once you see the process in action.

But most of all, someone has to let a child know that learning to learn is possible. Someone has to teach the child to recognize this process. That someone is you.

CHAPTER 16

Learning to Think: Metacognition

Well, you just make a picture in your mind and then you turn it around. If it doesn't seem to fit, then you try it the other way.

six-year-old girl

"Oh, help!" said Pooh. "I'd better go back."

"Oh, bother!" said Pooh. "I shall have to go on."

"I can't do either!" said Pooh. "Oh, help *and* bother!"

Now by this time Rabbit wanted to go for a walk too, and finding the front door full, he went out by the back door, and came round to Pooh, and looked at him.

"Hallo, are you stuck?" he asked.

"No, no," said Pooh carelessly. "Just resting and thinking and humming to myself."

'Here, give us a paw."

Pooh Bear stretched out a paw, and Rabbit pulled and pulled and pulled....

"*Ow!*" cried Pooh. "You're hurting!"

"The fact is," said Rabbit, "you're stuck."

"It all comes," said Pooh crossly, "of not having front doors big enough."

"It all comes," said Rabbit sternly, "of eating too much, I thought at the time."

A. A. Milne, *Winnie the Pooh*

In this chapter, I focus on the knowledge that young people have about thinking. There is definitely room for instruction in this area. We must teach young people how to think clearly, creatively, and efficiently. I envision an entire niche, a special, permanent, ongoing course, in the K-12 and in the higher education curricula, for instruction in how to learn, how to think, and how to enhance intelligence. This course must be aimed at focusing students' minds on the roles of various mental processes in intelligent thinking. Until such a subject becomes a basic part of all curricula, most individual teachers and parents are on their own: they must assume the responsibility for teaching children to think and to learn, as well as to learn to learn.

BASIC TYPES OF THINKING

Earlier I defined two different types of knowledge: expertise and control knowledge. Recall that expertise is also called material knowledge. Expertise is based on experience in the material, or outer, world. Its purpose is to know content—a body of specific facts. By contrast, control knowledge is based on what goes on in the mind. Its purpose is to know the process of thinking, to think about thinking.

Today, more than ever, knowledge is viewed as an elaborate system of processes instead of just a body of expertise or information. Thinking itself is viewed as a complex process. A growing emphasis is placed on the process of thinking, on control knowledge. We are indeed becoming increasingly conscious of what it means to think. We are turning our attention to the levels of thought that were once so automatic that we ignored them. Knowledge is encoded, put into a mental code, and then stored and operated on in the mind. This mental code is loaded with representations of the knowledge we store, categorize, later retrieve, and use or operate on.

If we can better understand children's (and adults') thinking processes, then we can teach them how to think and how to learn better. However, we must exercise caution in our efforts to mold children's mental processes. Whether it is in the form of parenting or teaching, we must be sensitive and always remember that we want to interact with and not intrude on the thinking process, that we influence and enhance the thinking process best by respecting the structure of the process.

What does it mean to respect the structure of the process? Your child accumulates a large quantity of experiences early in life. Your child builds experience-based notions of reality based on these experiences. Respect the child's experienced-based notions of reality. These experiences can affect your child's thought processes, ability to learn, and intelligence. Whether or not you or your child's teachers realize it, the process of educating a child involves interacting with the existing, experience-based notions of reality maintained by your child. Education that ignores these notions of reality does not educate. It does not retrain existing thought processes. It fights with them instead. And it often loses, leaving behind the damage it has caused, sometimes forever. Young people grow frustrated and even angry (sometimes only subconsciously but nevertheless very angry) when they sense this damage being wreaked. For many of them, the anger may never leave.

The education of children must talk to children's existing notions of reality. No matter how childish, immature, and naive these notions may seem, teaching is more effective when it works with them. Parents and teachers who proceed as if students' minds are devoid of all previous impressions will have little success. Too many errors are made in this way. All too often parents and teachers are tempted to assume that the reason for a student's incorrect answers is lesser mental ability or lower intelligence. This dangerous, all too prevalent assumption is based on parents' and teachers' lack of information about alternative knowledge structures, the existing notions of reality of children, teens, and adults.

Of note is the matter of the development of knowledge and reasoning in physics and related subject areas. Students' naive theories of physics affect their understandings of the laws of expert (or "real") physics. This means that the information a science teacher tries to teach often feels wrong to a child. Students arrive in their first physics classes not as blank slates in the areas of force and motion but with elaborate and quite naive theories of how things work and move (both conscious and subconscious theories). Although these elaborate theories describe and provide explanations for the behavior of moving objects, they support a host of misconceptions that actually run counter to the laws of physics. Some of these misconceived theories are similar to medieval explanations of force and motion. Many of these explanations have what seem to be childlike qualities in the eyes of expert physicists. Most of the naive explanations of force and motion are naïvetés shared by many people (including adults) who have not studied physics, who are not experts in physics.

I am providing some physics of simple force and motion as examples here, however this discussion applies to all areas of "how the world works" thinking. The naive explanations I am talking about are made up of specific misconceptions that are highly resistant to change even in the face of contradictory evidence. They have become embedded in the mental system at the perceptual-motor (gut) level rather than at an abstract (conceptual) level. What our children (and we) know about reality is based on our interpretations of our sensory experiences (and any illusions of these experiences). This includes those sensory experiences, or perceptions, I earlier explained when I talked about automatic illusion and not-seeing. And this interpretation of reality is not always correct. Circles that appear complete may not be complete. Bombs do not drop directly down from moving planes; they curve downward. Water does not gush from a coiled hose in a spiral; it shoots straight out. Yet many people (adults as well as children) who have had several courses in physics, frequently continue to insist that these things happen. Their reasoning is built upon what they believe they have seen to be true. Within their own private knowledge systems and realities, their answers are almost always, in their own minds, correct and logically derived.

Old belief systems die hard, when they can be put to rest at all. The process of changing a young person's mind about what is factual and accurate and real may require a great deal of experiential rethinking and reorganization of naïve or flawed beliefs about force, motion, and the makeup of the physical world in general. This experiential reorganization involves providing the young person experiences that are incompatible with her or his naive beliefs rather than simply saying "No, you are wrong about that," because this approach does not bring about a real change in thinking and knowledge. (Too much teaching, done by parents as well as teachers, simply shoves information at the child or teen, and this is not really teaching.) For example, saying, "Water does not come out of the coiled hose in a spiral," does not lead to a change in knowledge and thought processing in the young person's mind. Rather, showing the water coming out of the coiled hose perhaps more than once will lead to a reformulation of the thought process about how this works.

Proceed carefully. Returning to the water out of the hose example, if the young person thinks water gushes out of a coiled hose in a spiral, do not just explain why it does not. *Show* that it does not. When a young person is taught a new explanation for a physical event or for any other scientific, mathematical, or conceptual event, the teaching must build on what that young person already knows—even if what she or he knows is not correct. Parents and educators must respect the conflicts between knowledge structures that their children form as they develop (even if adults have no idea what these knowledge structures might be) and those they form as they learn that their (what some would call) "magical thinking" may not be accurate in all cases. Always keep in mind that what a child is being taught may be clashing with what the child thinks she or he already knows. Learning is adding to what one knows, building on it and reformulating it, not throwing it away. People of all ages can benefit by this realization. Parents do best with their children and teens when they understand this about themselves as well as about their children. (We can say the same for teachers, that they do best when they understand this about themselves as well as about their students.)

I want to underscore the importance of respecting existing knowledge structures no matter how naive rather than attacking them or destroying them or even only simply saying they are wrong. The internal, mental, and even emotional clash experienced by the young person faced with an adult (parent or teacher) shoving information at her or him (take this pill and swallow it) can result in anti-learning and resistance to reformulation of information. This clash is not always apparent, and its effects not always obvious. Still, this clash can take place, and we must be gentle with our young persons' learning processes.

Also note that what may seem to be lesser mental ability may actually be what I call the *anti-learning* coming out of the clash. It may also be the expression of intelligent but naive assumptions that are incorrect but have been formed (by the child or teen or adult you are working with) into rigid knowledge structures. With help, your child's mind can learn to evaluate and revise the knowledge structures it builds. Naive and alternate knowledge structures can be retrained, reformulated. In this way, intelligence or intelligent use of information can be learned.

Our understanding of the learnability of intelligence becomes clearer as we gain a better understanding of how knowledge is taken in and operated on by the brain. But can the mind learn? Can we really teach children to think about thinking? To learn to learn? Yes, we can. However, in so doing, we must always realize and respect the fact that a young person comes to any discussion about thinking with her or his own naive and often subconscious, but deeply ingrained, views on the subject.

PROBLEM SOLVING

For parents and teachers to help children learn to think, they must first do some thinking about their own thinking. Examine your own thought processes as well as those of others. Among the mental processes students, or any of us, can learn to work with is the all-important problem-solving process. Break this process down into as many distinct steps as possible. Here is my breakdown, based upon hundreds of interviews. You may have one of your own:

Step: Consider the reason or context for being presented with this problem.
Step: Assess the level of difficulty of this problem.
Step: Note your degree of familiarity with this problem, or with problems that seem like it.
Step: Judge the type of problem.
Step: See this problem in your mind.

(Continued)

Step: Try it on for size (physical imaging).
Step: Connect this problem to personal experience in the material world.
Step: Build on experience.
Step: Apply relevant principles.
Step: Break the problem into small steps.
Step: Build on others' findings.
Step: Build on your own findings after doing all of the above.
Step: Use everything available to you to think this through.

Do some thinking about each step that you identify. Ask yourself or the young person you are working with to do the following:

- *Consider the reason or context for being presented with this problem.* Why are you thinking about this problem right now? Did a teacher assign it to you? Did your parent give it to you to do? Did you find it in a book? Would you handle such a problem differently if you were working on it for a different reason?

- *Assess the level of difficulty of this problem.* How easy or difficult do you think this problem is? How do you know this? If you think it is too hard, are you responding to this problem first with your feelings (emotionally) before you just stop and think carefully about it? Can you tell the difference? This is a problem that you *can* think through to solve. Feelings are very useful, but the best feeling to have right now is one which says, "I *can* think this through clearly. I *can* think carefully about thinking, and I *do* want to think about problem solving."

- *Note your degree of familiarity with the problem, or with problems like it.* Have you been given a problem like this before? When? How often? Do you consider yourself used to, or just getting used to, or not very used to, or not at all used to, problems of this sort? What makes you think so? How do you know this?

- *Judge the type of problem.* Is this a math problem or a science problem or an English problem or some other kind of problem? How do you know what type of problem this is? What things about this problem tell you what kind of problem it is?

- *See this problem in your mind.* Make a picture of this problem, or something that looks like a part of this problem, in your mind. If you do not have a picture, just make one up. There is no right or wrong here. Any picture (or cartoon) in your mind is a good place to start.

Or, if you can draw or sketch something about this problem on paper, do this first. Then, try to see this sketch in your mind. What would it look like if you saw it on television? Now try to diagram this problem—in steps or phases—perhaps using boxes or circles, and lines and arrows in your diagram.

- *Try it on for size.* Imagine that you can walk into this diagram, image, or picture you have drawn. Wander around in it. How does it look from the inside? Can you see it from different corners or sides of the inside? What about from various sides of the outside? What we are talking about is physical imaging. We can use our imaginations to act out problems we are trying to solve—to see them. We can use our memories and our imaginations to act out things that we've done before with our bodies, in order to sense or visualize the answers to our questions. When we do this, we are engaging in physical imaging.

Look closely at what your own thinking about how something works really depends on. Can you think about other ways that this something might work? Can you see other ways in your mind? Treat it as if it were an object. If it is an object, ask yourself to imagine how it works. What steers it? What happens if you don't turn it on? What happens if it is upside down?

I find that the ease with which I can do physical imaging depends on whether the thing is familiar, something that I have done before. I reach into my data bank and look for a picture of what ever it is I am thinking about. Let's say it is a bicycle—I am wondering how a bicycle really works. I reach into my mind and I find a memory of myself riding the bike. I ride the bike in my mind.

- *Connect this problem to personal experience in the material world.* What sorts of things that you have done (games you have played, work you have done with your hands such as building or cooking or drawing or playing with toys) help you think about problems like this one? Explain how these are connected in your mind. What activity does this problem remind you of?

- *Apply relevant principles.* Are there specific rules or theories that you have been taught that are useful in thinking about this problem? If so, what are these? How do they apply?

- *Build on experience.* Use everything you know to help you solve this problem. Search through your mind for things that might help you, that you would tend to overlook.

- *Break the problem into small steps.* What do you do think first, second, third, and so on in solving this problem? What is the sequence of your thoughts? Think in small steps, specific pieces of the process.

- *Build on others' findings.* If you are working on this problem with another person, or persons, ask each other each of the above questions. Then build on each other's way of solving this problem.

- *Build on your own findings after doing all the above.* Once the above are under way or completed, then you have findings derived from all of the above efforts and other efforts in other arenas of your life. Build on these findings.

- *Use everything available to you to think this through.* This means exactly this: Use everything and every bit of information available to you to think this through.

RESPECT THE PROCESS

We can learn to recognize the particular reflexes (including emotions) that we and our children experience when confronted with particular mental tasks. If we can do so for ourselves, then we can help our children recognize their own responses to mental challenges.

Try to develop, in yourself and in the child, some degree of awareness regarding the mind's control of its knowledge and the knowledge process. Get, in as much detail as possible, the steps involved in thinking through a problem. Help the child become especially sensitive to:

- the emotions experienced when confronted with a mental problem
- the selection of a particular procedure for solving a problem
- the organization of the information about the problem
- the invoking of particular conventions in order to work on a problem (this may be visualizing or imaging a picture, or it may be some other procedure)

The goal here is not getting the answer but arriving at a clearer understanding of the process of getting the answer. Go for extremely specific knowledge of the process of solving whatever type of problem you are looking at. Aim for details. Be certain to tell a child, in the appropriate language for that child's age, "You have been able to bring some of the functional parts of answering such a question into your awareness, into words. Now listen to your mind. Your mind talks to you and you have to listen to it very carefully." Help the child incorporate the idea that the control knowledge I defined in the beginning of this book *is learnable* and that it is *a valuable thing to learn*.

REFORMULATION

As I noted earlier, the driving force behind all my research in the field of intelligence is my contention that intelligence, or mental competence, is learnable, and that modern K-12 and college curricula ought to regularly and directly address the learnability of intelligence. One of the central elements of such intelligence training should be exercises in reformulation.

The general purpose of a reformulation exercise is to take a child or teen (or adult) through a revision or reformulation of one of her or his naive (and "incorrect") theories. This teaches the child to examine and revise her or his own methods of thinking and problem solving, to learn to learn, and to let in new information. The goal is to expand the child's awareness of her or his own control knowledge. In your work with the child, you will have to select a vocabulary appropriate to that child's age. Aim to lead the child to:

- a greater consciousness of the workings of her or his control knowledge
- the belief that an awareness of one's own control knowledge is the first step in raising one's mental competence and intelligence
- a sense that control knowledge, and therefore at least one component of intelligence, is learnable

Select a problem to be solved or a question to be answered. Allow the child or teen (or adult) to give you an answer, even if it is incomplete or incorrect. In this case, you have more to work with if it is quite incomplete or incorrect. Direct the reformulation conversation in an increasingly introspective direction, getting to *exactly how* the child is thinking while trying to answer the question. Eventually, ask the original question again.

Let's say your original question is, "What makes a car run?" About two minutes into the discussion of how a car runs, explain that you are interested in your child's answers to this question, yes, and even more so in the mental processes she or he goes through while trying to answer. Ask the child what happens in her or his mind when you first ask the question, and what is happening in her or his mind after a while, which may be from three to five minutes after you first ask the question.

Then proceed to a new level of conversation in which you ask the child to report what she or he has to say about the question as well as what her or his mind is doing in order to answer the question. Ask, frequently, something like, "What is your mind doing now?" Continuously aim to reformulate, to increase the child's "grain" of understanding, to sharpen the child's focus on the workings of her or his own thinking process. This can be fun, and can even occur in casual play and conversation.

OBJECTIVES OF REFORMULATION

Experiment on an ongoing basis with your own and your child's reformulation processes. You will become an expert as you gain experience:

- *Encourage evolution of the knowledge system.* Rather than simply tell a child that she or he should reconsider or add to her or his definitions of intelligence, let the child observe her or his own mind at work. Encourage the child to draw into conscious observation her or his own mental workings, and then to build on a combination of what she or he already knows and what she or he newly observes. Ask: How is your thinking about this problem changing during this discussion?

- *Try to understand the intellectual topography.* Attempt to "climb inside" the mind of the child, to see the way that child sees the functioning of her or his own mind, and of the world.

- *Break mental problems into small pieces.* Aim to break down, into small manageable steps, not just the problem at hand (mathematical, scientific, and so on), but also the larger problem of explaining how a mind works when it encounters such a problem.

- *Keep the learning package small.* Do not take all aspects of thinking on at once. Focus on a single aspect of thinking (a single step or issue in algebra or in grammar, for example). Present one problem to solve at a time, to use as a demonstration. Being overwhelmed causes far too many problems to compound at once. Take these one step at a time.

- *Recognize what's important and not important, what's fundamental, and what's random in this process.* Wade through the many comments that do not pertain to control knowledge, always steering the conversation toward control knowledge or at least attempting to do so. Of course, you won't necessarily use the phrase "control knowledge" with children too young to appreciate it. Call it "thinking about how we think" or don't call it anything.

- *Apply a strategy to engage these fundamentals.* Listen closely for any indication of or reference to the controlling or performing of mental operations on material knowledge. Indications of this include:

  - any reference to the organization of ideas or facts in the mind
  - any reference to the classification of this problem as being in a particular subject or problem area
  - any reference to this problem as being a particular type of problem, similar to other problems
  - any direct or indirect reference to specific problem-solving methods

- *Note how easily a child will change formulations.* Although many children are prone to disagree about a new explanation, most are surprisingly willing to add new components to their own theories or formulations. The argumentation structures of children are not highly sound in resisting reformulation. This is especially true when children are invited to add to—rather than calling it revise or reformulate—their ideas about thinking and problem-solving. Their views regarding control knowledge or what they know of control knowledge are not at all resistant to reformulation. Perhaps this is because their own problem-solving theories, although seemingly complicated, are not highly developed along logical lines. (Just call it "adding to.")

The way a child (or an adult) organizes the process of solving a given problem is part of solving that problem. Quite often, we are not conscious of this level of our problem-solving activities. One reason that control knowledge is so frequently ignored is that it is not talked about. Furthermore, it may be inaccessible in the sense that the child (or the parent or the teacher) does not realize that control knowledge is indeed knowledge and that this knowledge can be put to good use. Knowledge processes are often subconscious. Young people suffer when their parents and teachers do not help them recognize these subconscious processes.

RECOGNIZE CRITICAL THINKING

We are fed, almost from day one of our lives, perceptions and definitions of reality. We are taught to accept much of this without question. Yet, our minds do question, whether or not we sense them doing so. On some level, we know how very subjective, and subject to revision, our ideas about reality might be were we to really question it all. But shaking things up feels somewhat risky, and asking if what we know is right feels like shaking things up.

We must understand, first about ourselves and then about our children, that we create our realities. We create our own thought processes. We actively select, whether we realize it or not, either consciously or subconsciously, the following control knowledge processes (all of which we can pull into our consciousness as we learn to think about our thinking):

- The specific problem-solving methods we apply to any given classroom or life situation.
- The method of labeling anything and everything fed to the brain from the sense organs, which is all just noise and scramble until it is labeled and organized by the brain.
- The processes of reasoning (thinking) through which we arrive at what seem to be simple, fundamental, and undeniable truths about reality, about procedures such as how to spell a word, how to add two numbers together, how to arrive at any basic conclusion such as the answer to any simple problem.
- The processes of abstract reasoning through which we arrive at answers to complex problems, based on all experiences we have had with everything to date.

We must also understand and teach our children that we have a choice as to how conscious we are of our mind's workings:

- Anything received by the brain is recognized when the brain has an existing slot for such data: for the type of data (this is a plant), for the data itself (this is a plant, a flower, even a flower of a particular type, a daisy). We might also say, "I recognize this problem—this is a type of math problem, a word problem, a word problem that consists of first an addition problem, then a subtraction problem."
- The brain determines the structure and organization of thought within the brain.
- Knowledge comes into existence by the recognizing, organizing, categorizing, processing efforts of the mind.
- The more elaborate these recognizing, organizing, categorizing, processing efforts, the more intelligent the resulting knowledge.

THINKING ABOUT THINKING

Even complex thoughts are built out of simple thoughts that are based on experience. Our understanding of *how able we are to think* and of *how we think* is based on experience—experience doing thinking. Let's take this to another level: Knowledge about one's own thinking—without the experience of thinking about one's own thinking—is not conscious experience-based knowledge about one's own thinking. (It may not even be knowledge at all, but let's save that discussion for another day.) Simply put: We must learn how to think. We must realize that we *can* learn how to think, because this empowers our thinking. We can make a point of consciously thinking about our thinking processes.

Learning *how* to think is much easier for people who were led into the process as children; however, adults can start at any time in life and still benefit from this activity. This is highly recommended, In fact, parents engaged in thinking about their own thinking processes can help their children understand this by modeling it. **Learning how to think is thinking well and thinking consciously.**

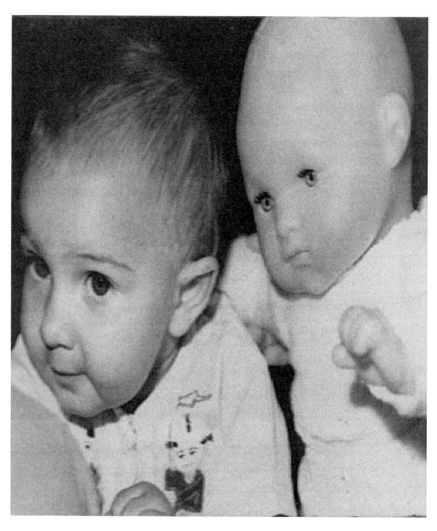

Thinking about Thinking (Courtesy of Angela Browne-Miller)

CHAPTER 17

The Role of Self-Esteem in Intelligence Enhancement

"O Tiger-lily!" said Alice, addressing herself to one that was waving grace-fully about in the wind, "I *wish* you could talk!"

"We *can* talk," said the Tiger-lily, "when there's anybody worth talking to."

Lewis Carroll, *Through the Looking Glass*

Whatever else is said about the enhancement of mental ability, self-esteem must not be overlooked. A young person's sense of self and respect for self can affect that child's expression of her or his mental ability. The better a child feels about her or himself, the better she or he may do with mental challenges. The lower a child's self-esteem, the more that child may stifle, suppress, and withhold high performance.

SELF-ESTEEM AND PERFORMANCE

Why does low self-esteem interfere with performance? The answer is most obvious when it comes to public performance, actions that involve being observed by other people (who are watching or just happen to notice). Whether it is being on stage, speaking in front of a group or a class, or rais-ing a hand for the teacher to call on, if a child feels unworthy or incompe-tent, that child may be reluctant to perform. If the child performs at all, the result will be less than the most the child can do.

The answer is much less obvious when we look at what we might call less public, more private performance. These include activities that are not done before the watching eyes of a group or a teacher or parent. More solitary activities such as writing alone, doing puzzles, and drawing can also be affected by low self-esteem. Although the child may feel less direct pressure in the absence of an audience, the child may nevertheless feel a silent pressure to perform and an unspoken sense that her or his performance will never be adequate. (Now, it is true that quite frequently a withdrawn child may entertain or occupy her or himself with gratifying activities or outlets such as drawing, writing long entries in a journal, or playing solitary games. The performance in this instance is secondary to the expression of self the child is seeking for her- or himself—self expression—in the absence of pressure from the outside world.)

Silent pressure comes from all directions. The first source of silent pressure is closely related to public performance pressure. If anyone will be evaluating the work (such as a teacher does when grading) or hearing about the quality of the work (such as parents do when they see report cards) or competing with the quality or grade assigned the work (such as do some classmates and some siblings), then the work or its results are going to become public performances. Knowing this, a child with esteem problems, or even a shy child, may be inhibited as if she or he might be on stage.

There are other sources of silent pressure. Even when the results of whatever the child is doing will not be witnessed or evaluated by teachers, parents, siblings, or classmates, the child may evaluate her or his own work much as a critical audience would. The child may have experienced evaluation in the form of grades or comments and may have been uncomfortable with it. The child may have taken in, internalized, the demand to do a good job from the social and family environment and then placed this expectation on her or his own work.

THE CHILD AS SELF-CRITIC

Many children become quite critical of themselves regardless of the support they glean from parents and teachers. Children are very perceptive and learn to make comparisons early in life. I remember when my daughter, at three and a half years of age, began comparing her own painting and drawing to mine. She insistently repeated that Mommy was better at painting than she, that she was not good at it. This was somewhat disconcerting, as I, in my love for drawing and painting, had shared my hobby with her regularly from an early age and her art work was highly vivid and complex for her age. I had never made any comparisons between her own and my own work, and I was always complimentary and encouraging. Eventually, she passed through this stage.

Parents must be sensitive to the rise of the inner critic in a child. This critic is sometimes so quite, so silent, so unspoken that parents may miss it. Parents must be sensitive to their children's experiences of criticism and or what may feel like criticism, even when there is none. Parents must also be sensitive to children's witnessing of parents' criticisms of each other, of themselves, and of other people.

TEACH "I CAN"

Early in life, children see, hear, and feel their parents' attitudes toward themselves. Children mimic much of what they see in their parents. So, parents' levels of self-esteem may have a great deal of influence on those of their children. If your child sees confidence and a sense of competence, the child may seek to mimic this. If the child sees fear, shyness, timidity, and a low sense of self-worth in the parent, the child may mimic this.

Children who see their parents, not necessarily as perfect or as high achievers, but as people who believe in themselves, who believe that they can, will learn this attitude. Parents who want to and try to teach their children to believe in themselves, to think positively, and to say "I can" instead of "I can't" must set an example.

Note that if you have not been setting the "I can" example, it is never too late to begin. You can teach your child a great deal by telling your child and showing your child that you have decided to change your attitude. You might say something like:

- "For a long time I thought I couldn't run two miles, but now I know that, if I want to, I can. I am writing a practice plan that starts me at one-half mile and has me at two miles by the end of the year."
- "I thought I was not a good speaker, but now I know that I can be a good speaker, I just need to practice before meetings, which I am starting now in little steps."
- "I thought I was a bad student when I was a kid, but I just did not know I could do the work, and now I know I can. I am going back to school and I know I can do a good job and pass all my classes."

RESTATE NEGATIVES INTO POSITIVES

Setting an example is one of the best ways to teach the "I can" attitude. While you are doing this, try another teaching method. This is the gentle restating of a child's negative statements into positive ones. Let's take a simple example to demonstrate the process. When you hear, "Mommy, I can't spell 'cat,'" you can say "How about saying this: 'I *can* spell cat, once I learn to.'" Do not do this in an argumentative, contradictory fashion. Simply restate, quietly, in a positive way, what has been said. If the child needs a demonstration of what you mean, demonstrate it. For example: You can make the sounds of each letter in cat, and help the child get the correct letter after each sound. When the child has spelled cat, compliment that child. Use the same approach:

- Restate it, whatever it is, in the positive: I can spell cat.
- Demonstrate that it can be done by trying again and again.

Eventually, your coaching on the spelling of cat, and later, on the spelling of other words, will be not be needed. Eventually, you will hear your child say, "I can spell 'cat.'" You may hear this even before the child spells cat entirely independently of you. Let this go, unless the child is repeatedly using the wrong spelling and thinking it is correct. (Then you will want to help the child with reformulating the spelling of this word before this spelling is embedded too deeply into the child's wrote memory. We return to reformulation itself later in this book.)

Whether it is spelling, writing, or adding or algebra or bicycle riding or using a computer or some other ability, your child needs to believe that it is possible for her or him to do it. As your child grows and learns certain tasks, no matter how small, applaud these achievements. You may think adding one plus two is easy and so may older children, but remember this is a big step for a child. Your approval is taken in by the child and is esteem-building.

FAILURE CAN BE LEARNING TOO

Failure is a part of the learning process. Some of us stumble, or even fall (or fail), more than others along the way. Each of us has our own life path to follow, and we walk our own special and often jagged learning curve. Children will learn to appreciate this view of life's challenges if you teach them to do so. Describe failure as a part of life, whether it is not passing a test or a grade, or just getting one word wrong. Understand that failure has a different meaning for each child. Note that even successful students can fail. A straight A student who gets her first B in twelfth grade may be deeply affected by this experience. Self-esteem is fragile in high achievers, as it is in all young people.

CHAPTER 18

Building People for Tomorrow

"That's a long time ago," said Wendy. "How time flies."

"Does it fly," asked Jane, "the way you flew when you were a child?"

Wendy smiled and said she sometimes wondered if she ever really did fly. But Jane was certain Wendy had. "Why can't you fly now?" she asked.

"Because I'm a grown-up now," said Wendy. "When people grow up, they forget. No one can fly when they grow up. You have to be young, innocent and a little selfish to fly."

J. M. Barrie, *Peter Pan*

This book offers parents, educators, and policymakers the view that young people's potential is highly moldable and not set in stone, that the mind and mental ability need not be stuck or left at any particular level. Early in this book, I explain some of the basic arguments relevant to this perspective that students, parents, teachers, philosophers, policymakers, and scientists make and are influenced by. Certainly, whether or not they realize they are doing this, parents and teachers must wade through all the theory and all the debate to choose what they think is valuable, and then to go on with parenting and teaching.

Parents must try to see themselves as their children's defense against institutions. No one has a greater interest in the success of an individual child than her or his parent. Until a child is old enough to protect her or his own interests in the development of her or his own mental ability, the parent must be the protector. Too many children get lost in the educational system, dropped or overlooked along the way. This is what the parent must try to prevent.

The parent must be the protector and then the advocate. Being the advocate means standing up for a child's right to learn, to realize her or his potential. Sometimes the parent must go to school and do the advocating. Sometimes the parent must do the advocating at home. There are so many social and psychological pressures on, and distracters affecting, a young person, that someone must advocate, day in and day out, year after year, for the development of that young person's mental potential.

WHAT I WANT TO BE

As I have said, parents are not alone in molding their children's minds. Siblings, friends, teachers, television, and so many other participants in children's lives have at least as much or even more influence, especially as children grow increasingly independent from their parents. Still, parents can remain quite central in the development of their children's and teens' mental abilities. And, always central (whether or not we consciously realize this) is the role parents play in the development of their children's and teens' *awareness* of their own mental abilities.

Parents have a huge opportunity here. After all, parents are the people that can, from very early childhood on, most help their children realize their own identities, their own power, their own abilities. How much of what a child thinks she or he can achieve can actually be achieved? Is a child really able to realize her or his dreams? Does the child dare to dream? Whether actively building answers or passively assisting in these areas, or doing nothing at all, parents are contributing a great deal to children's answers to such questions. Of course the world around the child has a great influence, and of course parents cannot make everything perfect and guarantee a child all she or he wants and needs; however, parents can set the stage for a child recognizing her or his own potential.

Given that even noninvolvement in developing a child's sense of power is negative involvement, a parent may as well elect to purposely contribute in a positive manner. This is more than the esteem-building discussed in earlier chapters. This is a conscious effort to share in the dream-building process, to let a child know that she or he can become a court reporter, a teacher, an athlete, an astronaut, an opera singer, a president—and most of all a satisfied, fulfilled adult, whatever form that may take.

A parent's most distinct effect on the child's sense of power is perhaps during the first nine or ten years of the child's life, when the parent tends to play the most central role in that child's life. These are the years when dreams about the future can still be aimed high and can still be underscored with confidence that they can come true. "What I want to be when I grow up" is as much reality as it is fantasy in these years. An artist, a singer, a fireman, a doctor, the president of the country—these are all still of equal possibility, if and only if a child has been exposed to these possibilities.

FEED THE DREAM

So how can adults feed children's dreams for their own futures? What kind of guidance works? Just about anything you do with the intent of guiding is guidance. Certainly this list is a good one to keep in mind:

- Get involved in this process of feeding good dreams at an early age.
- Have an "I can" attitude, about your own life as well about your child's life.
- Expose the child to a range of options. The life of your child belongs to your child, not to you. You can lead the child to the water of opportunity. You cannot make the child drink. But do provide the opportunity.
- Let the child know that you believe that much is possible with clear goals and the work to achieve those goals. Avoid saying, "You will never achieve that. You aren't good enough."
- Teach planning and organizational skills from the beginning. These skills blaze a clear trail through the jungle of stimuli, distractions, obstacles, challenges, and competing possibilities of life.

Feeding children's dreams requires demonstrating the process of making dreams come true. Do not in any way support the notion that just wishing to be a symphony conductor without studying music very seriously is possible. Explain that dreams can come true when we think clearly about how to get from the moment of now to the realization of the dream. There are many steps, real practical activities requiring real work, along the way. Let your child see this view demonstrated in her or his parents' and teachers' lives. Show your child how you go about realizing your dreams.

DEVELOPING YOUNG CHILDREN'S POTENTIAL

It is difficult to feed dreams of the future to underdeveloped minds. Parents and educators must begin empowering all children's minds, and begin even at very young ages. However, if the desire to empower a child comes to the parent when the child or teen is older, remember it is never too late. Again: IT IS NEVER TOO LATE. Most of the ideas in this book are relevant to children and teens—and even to adults—of all ages.

Early childhood is a very important time, as noted earlier. From birth to age three, a child undergoes intensive brain development: there are rapid connections among brain cells and related rapid growth of brain capacity. The first years of life are years in which the young mind is highly receptive to stimuli and to learning. It appears that approximately 80 percent of all the connections among brain cells may be formed by the age of three. Within the first six months of life, the child's brain capacity may reach 50 percent of its adult potential. By age three, this capacity may reach 80 percent of its adult potential. About the age of four, the primary developmental emphasis shifts away from the formation of sensory and neural pathways, the development of which has been occurring in the rear brain. Now comes the very important frontal lobe phase of the child's brain development. The connections formed during this phase are related to the cerebral "hardware" forged during the first three years of life.

The mental abilities being developed during this and later phases of mental development can and usually do reflect the nature and degree of earlier brain development. Again, the right stimulation during early childhood is so essential. This does not mean that later catching up is impossible, but it does mean that the time of life when the brain is more plastic and developing most rapidly is the optimal time for foundation-building.

Although there is remarkable and growing potential for later catching up, even catching up in adulthood, for making up for missed developmental opportunities, the task of catching up is demanding. Sometimes opportunity to catch up never arises. However, **catch-up is indeed possible**. My view is that we as a society must identify and seek these catch up opportunities, and make these opportunities available to those who require and desire this catch up; this will be of immense benefit to individuals as well as the entire population.

SUPERCHILD PRESSURE IS NOT THE ANSWER

The great cognitive potential of early childhood is not yet fully recognized. We do see that young children can learn to operate and program computers. Young children can learn an astounding array of complicated things: to play violin and piano through methods such as Suzuki's talent education, or Suzuki method, to solve intricate mathematical problems, to speak foreign languages, and, even before they can talk, to read their own, foreign, and even ancient languages.

As I mentioned earlier in my warnings about superchild consciousness, we must not get carried away here. An increasing number of parents feel far too much pressure to provide a concentrated preschool *education* instead of child *care* for their children so as to prepare them for the competition of later life. Special preschool programs, toys, computer programs, and parenting seminars have been established by responsive entrepreneurs who know about the pressures parents feel. What young children need most is good care. Some parents overlook affectionate attention in order to give their children what they believe are essential and actual educational advantages even before kindergarten. It is amazing what pressure and competition will drive parents to do.

Yet, some of the pressures parents feel are very real. The gap between children who have been exposed to intensive, professionally designed, "hi-tech" early education and those who have not is increasing. Frequently, I see the advantages that some children from some academic preschools have over children who did not have such preschool experiences. Do not let anyone tell you that it makes no difference what kind of mental stimulation a child receives in early childhood. It can make a difference. If the mental stimulation occurs in a group or school setting, the young child is gaining in two ways—via the stimulation and via the preparation for the social aspect of the school experience. However, stimulation that translates into pressure to achieve can be quite damaging in a child's early years. We walk a fine line here. These children's minds have so much unrealized potential. How do we unleash their mental abilities without breaking their spirits?

SOCIAL RESPONSIBILITY

Many people who are middle age and older adults today did not have the experience of an academic preschool, and have managed to find their way through adulthood. We cannot know whether their lives would have gone better or even differently had they had academic preschool educations.

A significant problem with being in favor of good early childhood (academic) education for all children is that not every child has access to it. My view is that we, as a nation, lose out by not lowering the start of public elementary school to the early childhood years. We lose too many minds, waste too many intelligences. We drain, or fail to develop, the intelligence of individuals—as well as of our society and of our species. (Note that prekindergarten or preschool could be made available to all, but left voluntary, while nevertheless being held accountable as a program in terms of academic quality. In other words, a parent who chose to stay home with the child could opt for this without the preschooler being held a truant. This is similar to the kindergarten option in many areas.)

School is part of the young person's environment. The expression of human intelligence is environmentally determined. To support this view, I have, in this book, discussed many attitudes and methods to promote the expression of ability. We must create a societal environment that maximizes the expression of the children's abilities without damaging the children while so doing.

Because a child's environment is such a powerful determinant of that child's expression of intelligence, we know that environment can change the outcome of a childhood, the outcome of an education, and even the outcome of a life. Given that environment plays such a powerful role in the development and expression of mental ability and even intelligence, the expression of intelligence and the social power it brings can and must be made available to all citizens by addressing the environmental aspects of intelligence development. Some environments encourage the development and expression of mental ability more than others. Why should this development and expression of mental ability remain restricted to only some portions of the population? Why should we not seek to ensure that every bit of ability there is among our population be developed and expressed? Isn't this in everyone's interest?

Of course, not only do we not make quality early childhood education available to all children, we do not make quality K-12 and higher education available to all citizens. Although some of this is surely a problem of access and social inequality, another large part of this situation is that we simply are not tapping into the massive knowledge we have regarding enhancing mental ability. So there is a political issue of the lack of equal educational opportunity for all, and there is the issue of our neglecting the massive intelligence-enhancing know-how and technology we already do have.

Why aren't we maximizing the expression of intelligence throughout our population, and why aren't the tools we do have being fully employed for everyone? The survival of the species may depend on our enhancing the intelligence of its members. Ensuring all citizens, including very young children, the absolute best education possible should be our primary policy priority. We must not go on wasting, failing to realize, the great potential of our children's minds.

A PARENT IS A TERRIBLE THING TO WASTE

And at the same time, we must realize how very precious parents are. Parents are the unseen heroes here. So often parents go unseen and unrecognized in their work to raise their children into adulthood. The survival and well-being of their children is their goal, and so often it takes every bit of energy and will to achieve these goals, or to even try to. It is quite often only decades later, when their children are adults and raising children of their own, that their children realize how very much their parents have done as their parents.

Parents are one of our greatest natural resources. The well-being and health of parents must become higher on our agendas. The survival of the child is linked to the survival of the parent. Parents bring in and raise the next generation, the future.

A parent is a terrible thing to waste, to not see in all this. Let us never forget the parent here.

A MIND IS A TERRIBLE THING TO WASTE

Yes, we have heard it said that a mind is a terrible thing to waste. Yet, how often do we avoid the implications of this adage in our own lives? A child's mind will develop as far as it thinks it can develop. This means that for a child to realize her or his own mental potential, that child must:

- be led to believe that the potential exists
- be encouraged to develop and realize this potential
- be provided the stimulation to develop this potential
- be provided the tools, training, and education to develop this potential
- be taught to see the rewards, the value, of mental development and of realizing one's mental potential
- be taught to examine the moral aspects of applying one's intelligence to a situation—for the good of all
- be taught the decision-making skills and social benefit aspects of moral intelligence

If you see to it that these elements are present, you can teach your child to realize her or his mental potential. This realization process is in itself intelligence. In fact, it is your responsibility to teach your child to always be becoming more intelligent, and to always be putting that intelligence to good work. Not only is this your responsibility to your child, but this is your responsibility to your society, your species, and your world.

Remember the old adage, "The way to a man's heart is through his stomach"? Well, our children are very hungry! Hungry for meaning, hungry for personal contact, hungry for opportunities to express what goes on in their minds. The ultimate way in to the child's mind is through the child's spirit. When a connection is made directly with the child's spirit, the mind can surpass even the greatest of expectations. We must guide our children and teens to fuller appreciation of, and desire for realization of, themselves. We must teach them to believe in their unlimited abilities. They must come to know that their abilities are worth developing. And worth continuing to develop throughout life.

Tempus fugit.

Epilogue

Walking Through the Gates of Knowledge

Many of the gates to educational and occupational opportunities once restricted to narrow elites have broken wide open. Many locks have come off, some easily and others after years, decades, even centuries of working at it. And we the people are charging through the gates. We are witnessing the expansion of rights to education, to learning, and to the opportunities these can bring.

There may still appear to be proportionately little room at the top. However, room at the top is expanding, and definitions of the top are widening. Opportunity is becoming, like necessity, the mother of invention.

Invention! Yes, the energetic human mind is creating opportunities that may not have yet existed or been recognized. And this is where we parents, teachers, and policy makers come in. We can nurture and energize the creativity that spots and even creates opportunities, that changes the room at the top and even the top itself. We can nurture and even energize the creativity and intelligence of children, teens, young adults—and of ourselves. We do have the simple tools and the essential drive to do this. This is our future we are nurturing.

We must make the development of the cognitive potential of our citizenry number one on our priority list. Simply put, our survival is at stake.

Yes, we have heard it said that a mind is a terrible thing to waste. Yet, how often do we avoid the implications of this adage? The care and feeding of all our young peoples' minds is some of the most important work we will ever do. It is some of the greatest love we will ever give. It is the guarantee of our freedom. Let's not keep the caretakers of the future unintelligent. We don't want them more susceptible to mindless acquiescence—to accepting the societal neglect of our intelligences as a given—do we?

Our Long Ride through Gates of Learning
(Courtesy of Angela Browne-Miller)

Bibliography

Adams, Gerald, ed. *Adolescent Development: The Essential Readings*. New York: John Wiley & Sons, 1999.

Aesop, *The Complete Fables*, trans. Olivia and Robert Temple. New York: Penguin, 1998.

Aguilar, Jemel P. "Adolescent Drug Sellers and Distributors." In *Praeger International Collection on Addictions*, ed. Angela Browne-Miller. Santa Barbara, CA: Praeger, 2009.

Allen, K. E., and Lynn R. Marotz. *Developmental Profiles: Pre-Birth through Twelve*. Belmont, CA: Cengage Delmar Learning, 2002.

Amen, Daniel G. *Magnificent Mind at Any Age: Treat Anxiety, Depression, Memory Problems, ADD, and Insomnia*. New York: Harmony Books, 2008.

Andersen, Hans Christian. *The Little Mermaid* (1837). In *The Little Mermaid: The Original Story*, ed. Charles Santore. New York: Random House Children's Books, 1997.

Bateson, Gregory. *Steps to an Ecology of Mind*. Winnipeg, Canada: Paladin Books, 1973.

Beck, Isabel L., Margaret G. McKeown, and Linda Kucan. *Bringing Words to Life: Robust Vocabulary Instruction*. Minneapolis: Guilford Publications, 2002.

Browne-Miller, Angela. *To Have and to Hurt*. Westport, CT: Praeger, 2007.

Brunelle, N., S. Brochu, and M.-M. Cousineau. "Drug-Crime Relations among Drug-consuming Juvenile Delinquents: A Tripartite Model and More." *Contemporary Drug Problems* 27 (2000): 835–866.

Brunelle, N., M.-M. Cousineau, and S. Brochu. "Juvenile Drug Use and Delinquency: Youths' Accounts of Their Trajectories." *Substance Use and Misuse* 40 (2005): 721–734.

Canfield, Jack, and Kent Healy. *The Success Principles for Teens: How to Get from Where You Are to Where You Want to Be*. Danbury, CT: Health Communications, 2008.

Carlson, Dale, and Hannah Carlson. *Where's Your Head? Psychology for Teenagers.* 2nd ed. Madison, CT: Bick House, 1998.

Carroll, Lewis. *Through the Looking Glass.* Danbury, CT: Digital Scanning, 2007.

Carroll, Lewis, and John Tenniel. *Alice in Wonderland.* Danbury, CT: Digital Scanning, 2007.

Childmark. "Five Ways to Stimulate Your Baby's Eyesight." September 1, 2008. http://www.childmark.com/blog/5-ways-to-stimulate-your-babys-eyesight.

Collodi, Carlo. *Pinocchio: The Story of a Marionette.* New York: Macmillan, 2002.

Coons, Arthur. *Crises in California Higher Education: Experience under the Master Plan and Problems of Coordination, 1959–1968.* Los Angeles: Ward Ritchie Press, 1968.

Covey, Sean. *The Seven Habits of Highly Effective Teens: The Ultimate Teenage Success Guide.* New York: Simon & Schuster, 1999.

Damon, William, and Richard M. Lerner. *Child and Adolescent Development: An Advanced Course.* New York: John Wiley & Sons, 2008.

Dispenza, D.C. *Evolve Your Brain: The Science of Changing Your Mind.* Deerfield, FL.: Health Communications, 2007.

Douglass, John Aubrey. "Brokering the 1960 Master Plan: Pat Brown and the Promise of California Higher Education." *California Politics and Policy, Special Issue* (1997).

———. *The California Idea and American Higher Education: 1850 to the 1960 Master Plan.* Stanford, CA: Stanford University Press, 2000.

———. "A Tale of Two Universities of California: A Tour of Strategic Issues Past and Prospective." *Chronicle of the University of California* 4 (2000).

Eliot, Lise. *What's Going on in There? How the Brain and Mind Develop in the First Five Years of Life.* New York: Bantam, 2000.

Elliot, Orinn Leslie. *Stanford University: The First Twenty-Five Years.* Stanford, CA: Stanford University Press, 1937.

Gardner, Howard. *Changing Minds: The Art and Science of Changing Our Own and Other People's Minds.* Boston: Harvard Business School Press, 2006.

———. *Frames of Mind: The Theory of Multiple Intelligences.* New York: Basic Books, 2004.

———. *Intelligence Reframed: Multiple Intelligences for the Twenty-First Century.* New York: Basic Books, 2000.

Goleman, Daniel P. *Social Intelligence: The New Science of Human Relationships.* New York: Bantam, 2006.

———. *Working with Emotional Intelligence.* New York: Bantam, 2000.

Good, Diane L. *Brown v. Board of Education: A Civil Rights Milestone.* New York: Power Kids Press, 2004.

Grabarek, Krzysztof. "Staying Involved: Approaches to Helping." Parent Academic Resources, Inc. http://www.academicresources.org/learning.html.

Grahame, Kenneth. *The Wind in the Willows.* New York: Scholastic Paperbacks, 1987.

Healy, Jane M. *Your Child's Growing Mind: Brain Development and Learning from Birth to Adolescence*. New York: Broadway Books, 2004.

Jung, Insung. "Internet-Based Distance Education." College of Education, Pennsylvania State University. http://www.ed.psu.edu/acsde/annbib/annbib.asp.

Kirp, David L. *The Sandbox Investment: The Preschool Movement and Kids-First Politics*. Cambridge, MA: Harvard University Press, 2007.

Klingsberg, Torkel. *The Overflowing Brain: Information Overload and the Limits of Working Memory*. New York: Oxford University Press, 2008.

Kubey, Robert W. "Addiction to Television: With Commentary on Dependence on Video Games and the Internet." In *Praeger International Collection on Addictions*, ed. Angela Browne-Miller. Santa Barbara, CA: Praeger, 2009.

Lussier, Isabelle D., Jeffrey L. Derevensky, and Rina Gupta. "Youth Gambling Prevention and Resilience Education: A Harm Reduction Approach." In *Praeger International Collection on Addictions*, ed. Angela Browne-Miller. Santa Barbara, CA: Praeger, 2009.

Lynch, K. B., S. R. Geller, and M. G. Schmidt. "Multi-year Evaluation of the Effectiveness of a Resilience-based Prevention Program for Young Children." *Journal of Primary Prevention* 24 (2004): 335–353.

Maeroff, Gene I. *Building Blocks: Making Children Successful in the Early Years of School*. New York: Palgrave Macmillan, 2006.

Marzano, Robert J. *Building Background Knowledge for Academic Achievement: Research on What Works in Schools*. Alexandria, VA: Association for Supervision and Curriculum Development, 2005.

Masten, A. S. "Ordinary Magic: Resilience Processes in Development." *American Psychologist* 56 (2001): 227–238.

Masten, A. S., K. M. Best, and N. Garmezy. "Resilience and Development: Contributions from the Study of Children Who Overcome Adversity." *Development and Psychopathology* 2 (1990): 425–444.

Miller, Jake. *Brown v. Board of Education of Topeka: Challenging School Segregation in the Supreme Court*. New York: Power Kids Press, 2004.

Mosher, J. "Transcendental Alcohol Marketing: Rap Music and the Youth Market." *Addiction* 100 (2005): 1203–1204.

Neihart, Maureen, Sally M. Reis, Nancy M. Robinson, and Sidney M. Moon, eds. *The Social and Emotional Development of Gifted Children: What Do We Know?* New York: Prufrock Press, 2001.

Parton, Dorothy M. *The Open Door College: A Case Study*. New York: McGraw-Hill, 1960.

Pasamanick, B., and A. M. Lilienfeld. "Association of Maternal and Fetal Factors with Development of Mental Deficiency: Abnormalities in the Prenatal and Paranatal Periods." *Journal of the American Medical Association* 159 (1956): 155–160.

Peacock, R. B., P. A. Day, and T. D. Peacock. "Adolescent Gambling on a Great Lakes Indian Reservation." *Journal of Human Behavior in the Social Environment* 2 (1999): 5–17.

Petry, N. M. "Prevention: Focus on Gambling in Youth and Young Adults." In *Pathological Gambling: Etiology, Comorbidity, and Treatment*, ed. N. M. Petry, 269–278. Washington, DC: American Psychological Association Press, 2005.

Pressley, Michael, and Christine B. McCormick. *Child and Adolescent Development for Educators*. Minneapolis: Guilford Publications, 2006.

Pruitt, David B. *Your Adolescent: Emotional, Behavioral, and Cognitive Development from Early Adolescence through Teen Years*. New York: HarperCollins, 1999.

Shelov, Steven P., and Robert E. Hannemann, eds. *Caring for Your Baby and Young Child: Birth to Age Five*. New York: Bantam, 1998.

Zigler, Edward, Walter Gilliam, and Stephanie Jones. *A Vision for Universal Preschool Education*. New York: Cambridge University Press, 2006.

Index

About the Author

Author, lecturer, educator, psychotherapist, social scientist, mother, Dr. ANGELA BROWNE-MILLER earned her two doctorates (one in education and one in social welfare) and two masters degrees (one in public health and one in social work) at the University of California, Berkeley, where she lectured in three departments for over a decade. Angela has served as a U.S. National Institute of Mental Health Postdoctoral Fellow, a U.S. Administration on Children Youth and Families Fellow, and a U.S. Public Health Department Fellow. She has taught and designed curricula for learners at all levels, ranging from early childhood through midrange childhood, adolescence, young adult, adult of all ages, and senior citizen. She has studied closely cognitive, psychosocial, and emotional learning processes and the varying learning modalities involved in learning and retention at all ages; overcoming patterns of nonlearning (at all ages); and enhancing learning and even intelligence in children, teens, and adults. She has also worked with several thousand persons of all ages, on the above listed and other cognitive-psycho-socio-emotional issues, in clinical settings including her own private practice. Dr. Browne-Miller is director of the Metaxis Institute for Personal, Social and Systems Learning and Change in Northern California. She can be reached at www.AngelaBrowne-Miller.com.